# A Sister's Promise

## Judy Barber

The opinions expressed in this manuscript are solely the opinions of the author and do not represent the opinions or thoughts of the publisher. The author has represented and warranted full ownership and/or legal right to publish all the materials in this book.

A Sister's Promise
All Rights Reserved.
Copyright © 2015 Judy Barber
v1.0

Cover Photo © 2015 Judy Barber. All rights reserved - used with permission.

This book may not be reproduced, transmitted, or stored in whole or in part by any means, including graphic, electronic, or mechanical without the express written consent of the publisher except in the case of brief quotations embodied in critical articles and reviews.

Outskirts Press, Inc.
http://www.outskirtspress.com

ISBN: 978-1-4787-4687-4

Outskirts Press and the "OP" logo are trademarks belonging to Outskirts Press, Inc.

PRINTED IN THE UNITED STATES OF AMERICA

This book is dedicated to my loving sister
*Cher*

I will never forget the words that changed my life forever 'THEY FOUND CHER'S BODY". I remember just screaming and screaming asking WHY WHY DID IT HAVE TO BE CHER!!!!!!!! I found myself in a fog, unclear of what was happening. I was planning on visiting Cher for the first time in her paradise. We talked about what we were going to do and where we were going to go. This cannot be real. I felt that if I screamed loud enough that somehow it would change what I just heard. I remember being on my front porch and looking up at the sky and screaming CHER CHER NO WAY NOT CHER!!!!!!! I did not understand and still to this day do not understand why this had to happen.

*Cher at what she said was the most peaceful place she knew*

## JUDY BARBER

Cher was the oldest of five children and I am her baby sister Judy. I am writing this book as a tribute to my sister. I can only think by writing her story, the world might have the chance to know her. She was only fifty three when she was murdered by a serial killer. Cher touched a lot of lives and had many friends. It was a miracle that we were able to find out what happened to her. We were not about to let her just disappear. These are actual emails and daily events that happened. As you will see from the emails in the story, there were a lot of people looking for her. She meant a lot to so many people and we all miss her.

Cher and I were close. She was always there to watch out for me.

We spent many years together and stayed in contact when we were apart. I always looked up to my big sister and was so proud of her. She was a successful business woman that had accomplished her dreams. She knew how to work hard and she took the time to enjoy her life as well. She showed me a part of life I will always cherish. The memories I have are priceless. I am so thankful to have had the time I did with her. I am so thankful to be able to say I am Cher's baby sister.

We did not have the best of childhoods growing up in St. Louis Missouri. At one point when we were still young kids we moved to the country to the town of Fletcher. We had a three room log cabin on ten acres of land. We had no running water and an OUT HOUSE!!!!. There were five kids (four girls and one boy), our mom, step dad and his brother. Since we only had three rooms all of the kids slept in the attic. We had a few mattresses on the floor to sleep on. You could only stand in the middle of the attic or you would hit your head. We had to adjust to the farm life. Taking care of the cows, pigs, chickens, a rabbit, horse and miniature schnauzers. It was to say the least an adjustment coming from a nice neighborhood and a large house with a pool. I feel like going through that as a child was what prepared Cher to be able to adjust to going to a different country such as Panama and doing without the precious items that we so seem to need in the United States. Cher was the first one to leave the farm and she moved in with our father. She worked different jobs including six flags and doing some modeling. She learned at an early age how to support herself and be an independent woman. I got pregnant at the age of fifteen and had my daughter 6 months after I turned sixteen. I was young and not sure what to do with my life other than I knew I wanted to keep my child.

Cher fell in love and married her first husband Joe. I married my first husband Jim. We were both busy in our own lives but still had contact with each other. Cher's marriage was rocky and her husband moved to Florida.

Over the years Cher still had this restless side that wanted to get out of Missouri. Her husband was in Florida and she wanted to be with him. Cher was moving to Florida in 1987 and knew that I was in an abusive marriage and I was not happy. I will never forget her coming to see me and saying "I am moving to Florida in two week you want to come with me?" I was scared and had never been to Florida but I trusted her and wanted a better life. I was too afraid to tell my husband I was leaving so we had to find a way for me to leave without him knowing. Cher loaned him the money to go to court and pay a ticket and I moved to Florida. Cher arranged for the moving truck to be down the road from where I lived and to wait on me. I called on friends to help me pack the three bedroom trailer while my husband was gone. Much to my surprise we were done in one hour. We put everything into everyone's vehicles, meet the moving truck and loaded all my stuff. Cher and I then went to my daughter's school and picked her up. We told my daughter we are moving and going to live together in Florida. Jennifer was not happy at first but twenty minutes in the car with Cher and we are singing at the top of our lungs. We were on our way out of Missouri. Off to our new adventure and new life in Florida.

Cher got a job as a bartender and I worked at a stock brokerage company. We were together every day. She took my daughter Jennifer with her all the time. They were very close. My daughter was only eight at the time and she so admired her aunt Cher. Cher would always dress her so cute and everyone thought Jennifer belonged to Cher.

Of course Cher was a big kid herself and would let Jennifer do things that I would not. I remember a few weeks after we moved to Florida we went to a festival on the beach. There was a hula hoop contest that was announced over the intercom system. The prize was a hundred dollars' worth of ice cream. Well Jennifer was begging me to let her enter the contest. When we got close to the stage I could see there was a lot of girls in their twenties with their bikinis on that were going to compete. I told Jennifer that I did not think it was a good idea. Cher and Joe had a different view and convinced me to let her enter. Well there we were standing there watching Jennifer hula hoop like I never knew she could. It got down to Jennifer and a girl in her twenties. Cher started chanting JENNIFER, JENNIFER and before you knew it the crowd was joining in. The crowd began to grow and I could barely see Jennifer. The other girl dropped the hoop after a good fifteen minutes and Jennifer won. Someone from the crowd rushed to Jennifer and put her up on stage. She was so excited and wanted that hundred dollars' worth of ice cream. When I got her off the stage she looked at me and said "I told you I would win that ice cream". Cher just looked at me and smiled that smile she had. She high fived Jennifer and said "That's the way to show them and we will be eating ice cream for a long time."

It was just one of the many moments that I hold so dear and am so thankful that I had with Cher. Cher loved kids but never had any of her own. We always had the neighborhood children at our house. They were not there to play with Jennifer they were there to see Cher. Jennifer had her friends but Cher just seemed to attract any kid that walked by. All the kids called her aunt Cher. She loved that and loved having young kids around and laughing and playing like she was a kid herself. Cher and her husband Joe wound up getting a divorce and Cher took over the sign business they had. She ran the business for sixteen years and became very successful. She was able to not only run the business but she would actually drive her bucket truck and install huge sign faces herself. She was a smart business woman and invested her money in real estate. She met Dave along the way and she fell in love. They were the Ken and Barbie of St. Pete. They spent many years together living life to the fullest. I met my husband Doug and also fell in love. We got married September 4th 1999. Cher and Dave invited myself, Doug and my daughter Jennifer to go on a boat ride from Miami to a little island in the Bahamas to celebrate the millennium. There was ten of us that went on two boats. It was the most amazing time. Just seeing how the people lived on such a small island and they were so content with life. I believe this was the first taste for Cher of what she wanted for her future. Dave and Cher had a chance to go visit a place in Panama with some friends and that is where they decided they wanted to live out the rest of their lives.

Knowing Cher and how much children meant to her it was no surprise that she would fall in love with the children of Bocas Del Toro Panama. Cher would have movie night at her place once a month and invite the children to come. She would make popcorn and sit with them and watch TV. Some of the children did not have the luxury of having television. She would also have a girl's day and they would paint their fingernails and toes. I even was told the story of Cher having an Easter egg hunt. The children of Bocas had never seen colored eggs and had no idea what she was doing hiding the eggs. I know she left a lasting impression on those children that they will remember forever. There was just something magic about her and it showed whenever she was around little children. The more children around her the better she liked it. I am proud to share the photos of her with the children of Bocas and the story of her love.

Cher and Dave spent many happy years together in Panama. They would come and visit often and tell us all about the life there. As with any other couple they had their issues. Cher and Dave eventually separated. Cher came to visit me in October 2009 and it was the first time that I was able to give her the hug and the love that she needed. She was very upset over the breakup with Dave. She cried many nights while I held her in my arms and told her I loved her and was there for

*Cher enjoying the kids of Bocas.*

## A SISTER'S PROMISE

her. This is something Cher had done for me for many years and helped me through many rough times. She was always there to rescue me no matter where I was or where she was. Cher was really devastated that her relationship seemed over. She asked me to promise that if anything happened to her that she would be buried on her island and also buried on Sunshine Island in Florida. Of course I said "I PROMISE". I had no idea that it would not be long before I would have to full fill that promise. I celebrated her birthday November 15th with her which at the time I did not know that would be the last one she ever had. Cher just turned fifty three. We made plans for me to go to panama. My marriage to Doug was not going that well. I wanted to be with Cher. If I liked it then I would move to panama and run the motel for her. We would be together again just like old times. My heart and head where finally ready to take this chance and hopefully find the life I have been wanting. I had something to look forward to. Could this be a new chance in life again given to me by Cher? YES YES YES!!!!!!!!!!!!!!

*Cher in my bedroom in St. Petersburg, Florida October 2009*

*Celebrated Halloween together. Cher, Jennifer my daughter and me.*

*Celebrated Cher's birthday. The LAST ONE!!!!!!!!*

# A SISTER'S PROMISE

We went to Rib Fest during the day November 15, 2009. We went to the beach bar birthday night.

I AM SO THANKFUL TO HAVE SHARED THIS TIME TOGETHER!!!!!!

Cher was getting ready to go back to Panama and went to the Don Cesar to say Goodbye to Keli. This would be the place that we held Cher's Service.

*Cher at the Don Cesar before she left for Panama*

# A SISTER'S PROMISE

When she went back to panama I was all about getting myself together and getting ready for my new life. I was emailing Cher all the time. Checking up on her and letting her know that I am coming soon.

## November 25th, 2009 11:12 p.m. I joined face book to stay in contact with Cher

Judy and Cher Hughes are now friends.

## November 26th, 2009 I received a face book message from Cher

Sent: Thursday, November 26, 2009 8:40 AM
Subject: Cher Hughes wrote on your Wall...

Cher posted something on your Wall and wrote:

"hello happy thanksgiving so glad you are on face book...i am at island and trip was good went out with friends monday night and had a lot of fun...hows the shower"

## November 26th, 2009 8:45am Mary wrote on my face book wall

Mary wrote on your timeline.
"HEY JUDY!! Have a Happy Thanksgiving!"

## November 28th, 2009 I emailed Cher back

Sent: Saturday, November 28, 2009 4:01 PM
Subject: judy

hey how are you doing? i got on face book but afraid to write on there & let everyone see.

jen & i went to my friend roxanne's for turkey day. doug went with roger. roxanne told me she had called here for me and he cried to her for over a half hour. she told him well doug when you were sick judy was always there for you and now that you got better you left her sit. what else can you say.

are you taking care of yourself? email me and let me know how you are.

i miss you and love you.
judy

I remember letting Cher know that I was going to get my teeth fixed so I could have a great smile to go with my new life.

## November 30th 2009 I received a face book from Cher

**horay for judy**
i can see your smile from here...good for you, i am in bocas and going to island tomorrow, glad you are good....big love right back at you

This sticks in my head and haunts me still. The fact that she never got to see my new smile in person is heartbreaking.

We stayed in contact by face book and email. We were both so excited and needed each other to keep our spirits up.

## December 3rd, 2009 I sent Cher a face book message

hey how are you doing? i hope all is well. same ole thing here. just getting home from work. i'm back on the south beach diet and i have lost 4 1/2 pounds since monday. things are ok here, still dealing with the pain in my ass but it will be coming to an end so i can't dwell on it. i miss you. i really did enjoy seeing you. looks like from your pictures your doing ok. just remember we made it thru before and we will make it thru again.

i hope this is the way to send this. i'm still learning. my friend at work said if you post something on the wall everyone can see it but if you do the send a message it's just like an email. let me know. love ya & miss ya

i just poked you????? hope it didn't hurt. LOL

## December 3rd, 2009 Cher sent me a message back on Face book

Sent: Thursday, December 3, 2009 9:55 PM
Subject: Cher Hughes sent you a message on Face book...
Cher sent you a message.

Re: judy

"glad to hear from you i am ok and miss you too...you ara invited to a boat parade party at julies house and jen....love to you cher bear"

Sent: Thursday, December 3, 2009 9:56 PM
Subject: Cher Hughes sent you a message on Face book...

Cher sent you a message.

## JUDY BARBER

Re: judy

"you know i didnt feel a thing....guess i got hard haha lol"

## December 5th, 2009 I sent a face book message to Cher

Hey Sis,
how are you. i need to take a day off work and get my passport & file my divorce papers and make a doctor appointment and get it done. i have a floating holiday since i worked the friday after thanksgiving. i really have been thinking about getting the heck out of here and taking a fricken break from this place or leaving and never coming back. email or call me when you get a chance. love ya

## December 6th, 2009 sent an email to Cher and Mary

Sent: Sunday, December 6, 2009 4:26 PM
Subject: FW: 52 things you would love to say out loud at work:

Hi
thought i would share this, it's pretty funny. hope you both are doing well. COME ON APRIL i'm so looking forward to being together again. LOVE YA

## DECEMBER 8th, 2009 I FILED FOR DIVORCE

## December 8th, 2009 I received a face book message from Cher

Sent: Tuesday, December 8, 2009 6:06 PM
Subject: Cher Hughes sent you a message on Face book...

Re: judy

"hey i am not good...really a mess.....i saw Dave out the corner of my eye..at a bar and i spoke with him on the phone and he just screamed at me...i did not get to talk at all...and he has turned everything around.....and everything is my fault now....i am exausted...with his tricks"

## December 9th 2009 I emailed Cher

Sent: Wednesday, December 9, 2009 8:11 PM
Subject: judy

Hey hang in there. it will get better. i filed for my divorce yesterday morning at 8 am when the office opened. i had a flat tire on monday so i took jens car and then left work after my 8 hours cause i had a really bad day. i'm waiting for the sheriff to serve him the papers. they have 48 hours to serve him. so they should be coming soon. call me when you get the chance. BELIEVE ME AFTER ALL WE HAVE BEEN THRU IT WILL GET BETTER OR WE WILL JUST GET TIRED OF THEIR SHIT.

I LOVE YOU AND MISS YOU.

## December 10th, 2009 I received an email from Cher

Sent: Thursday, December 10, 2009 11:59 AM
Subject: Re: judy

hello baby...wow hope you are ok.... Dave is allover me tooo....he said that i am the one person that has treated him badly in his life.....what ever.....are you ok.....mine is coming to a head also....wow hope you feel better.....i know you do....i love ya.....

## JUDY BARBER

i am so lonely here.... John is back and is trying to help me...which i appreciate...got a freezer working so it will be better to stay here.....as i have not had enough electric to watch tv....and then Dave is being the devil again...

well for now i leave you with some love....big love cher

## December 10th, 2009 I emailed Cher

Sent: Thursday, December 10, 2009 7:55 PM
Subject: JUDY

Hey Sis,
doug got served the papers today. he is sitting in the garage on the phone with his girlfriend reading her the papers so SHE can explain them to him. WOW I'M SO GLAD SOMEONE ELSE HAS TO EXPLAIN THINGS!!!!! i'm ok NO I'M GREAT. CRAZY!!!!!!! i truly do realize that i have had enough of other peoples shit and it is TRUELY MY TURN.

i love ya & miss you. please take care of yourself as well. i am ready to begin my life. THINGS ARE LOOKING UP.
write back soon.

## December 11th, 2009 I received an email from Cher

Sent: Friday, December 11, 2009 8:02 AM
Subject: Re: JUDY

judy, good for you....and you are right....things are looking up....i am sooooo lonely...its horible...last night cryed myself to sleep again.... was suposed to talk with Dave on the phone....he wants his stuff really bad...

i sent him a message text....that i was on a beautiful island and in the middle of a nightmare fairytale and had a idea he would not want to hear what i had to say, so if it was ok with him i was gonna drink myself to sleep and another time to talk would be better for me ...sorry cher bear.....so thats what i did....he sent me a text back that said well you wanted to own it all so i should enjoy so i sent another you dont understand all fairytales have 2 very hot people in them.....

glad u r better....big love to hope i make it though all this....love cher

Sent: Friday, December 11, 2009 8:03 AM
Subject: Re: JUDY

oh what did the papers say...he gets nothin or something and get out or what...you could still keep him for a roomate.....cher

## December 13th, 2009 I emailed Cher

Sent: Sunday, December 13, 2009 5:08 PM
Subject: judy

hey,
the papers say that he gets the truck but has to register & put insurance in his own name, i get the house and the credit card debt. he has twenty day to respond. i can make him move after that. i need the roommate right now but i'm telling you he gets on my nerves and his liars are sickening. went out friday night with jen to banana boat stayed till closing. met a guy named brian that loves to dance, so you know me i danced my ass off. he was good too. left him when the bar closed and a couple friends came over and we were up until 6 am. last night i met about twenty people from work at a gay bar and watched the drag show. we had a blast!!!! we danced and played pool and just had a great night. we are doing it again for sure. i really

## JUDY BARBER

needed the outlet. i spent many night crying myself to sleep too and i think it is just a healing process. it will get better and you will get stronger. i keep looking at doug and thinking why did i put up with your shit for so long? no more, it's gonna be my way or the highway. well hang in there and i love you and send you a big big huge. love you talk to you soon. Judy

### December 14th, 2009 I received and email from Cher

Sent: Monday, December 14, 2009 9:33 AM
Subject: Re: judy

hello went out in bocas to rocky horror picture show wait till i put these photos on ...you wont beleive it....really had fun too...thanks for hope...i am still very sad....but getting better....i dont want to spend christmas alone...but have a friend...julie want's you to come to her house for party tonight...you should go....you will have fun....she is having a chocolate fountain ...go you should tell everyone hello and i love them ..i wish i was with you....we were good for each other.... hey jen....lol cher

### I emailed Cher back

Sent: Monday, December 14, 2009 7:06 PM
Subject: judy

hey there, glad you are going out and having fun. YOU DESERVE IT. i had a really good time with the people i work with. that's all we talked about today was when are we going to do it again. we had our pot luck lunch and everyone brought something good to eat. then we exchanged our secret santa gifts. i got a couple of candles and some candy. if you have candles over there you need to get one called cranberry mandarin IT SMELLS AWESOME. it's a walmart brand called MAINSTAYS. not sure if you can get it there. everything else is still the same around here. just taking it day by day. i talked to debbie my friend in mississippi and she said to tell you "HI" i told her she needs to get to feeling better so she can come see me and then we'll come see you. i really do want to come and already filled my passport info out and printed it today. i had to take a day off because i had to work the day after thanksgiving so i had a floating holiday i had to use within 30 days. i am taking friday off, not sure if i'm telling anyone in the house. why can't there just be a guy that is not a pain!!!!!

well gotta go for now. i love ya & miss you. write back soon Judy

## December 17th, 2009 sent an email to Cher

Sent: Thursday, December 17, 2009 7:07 PM
Subject: judy

hey sis,
how are you? just getting home from work. i have tomorrow off so i am drinking a beer all alone. wish i was having a few with you. i plan on going to get my passport tomorrow so i can come in april. are you hanging in there ok? i know it's frickin ruff. i hate my life sometimes. i really wish i had someone to celebrate my day off with.
well email me back so i know your ok.
love ya
judy

## Sunday December 20th, 2009 sent an email to Cher

Sent: Sunday, December 20, 2009 5:13 PM
Subject: judy

## JUDY BARBER

hey sis,
haven't heard from you in a while. you doing ok? i'm hanging in there. went christmas shopping today with jen. of course she wanted to get doug a few things and it broke my heart. i was in the store trying not to cry. i had to take a half a zanax to stay calm. it's hard to shop for someone i loved so much and now has taken my heart and broke it. jennifer was writing a list of things for doug to get us and i told her to write down i want my heart back. why does life have to be so unfair? i feel really lonely and i know you do to. all i ever wanted was someone to love and share the REST of my life with. i guess nothing last forever especially love. i feel so fricking empty. i was watching everyone shopping and having fun and to me it was a torture that i almost couldn't take. but i got it done and know i have to deal with it. WHY can someone please tell my WHY we have to go thru this?
it really suck sometimes. the only thing i can look forward to is going to work. i hope you are handling your situation. i know how tuff it is. i feel so bad for you too. all the pain we have had our entire life and it never seems to end. THIS SUCKS. i really hope you are ok. please write me back and let me know how you are. you said you would stay in touch so you have to write me. it's ok if you just need to vent. HELL I JUST DID. i have to have someone to tell this to. i know you understand. just remember i'm here for you always.
i love you and i miss you. waiting to hear from you.
love judy

## December 27th 2009 I received another inspiring face book from my big sister.

merry christmas sweetie....i spent it with 5 girls and had a blast...going to columbia for a week or two ...but will try to keep you abreast of whats up....i m putting a foot infront of the other....going diving too....i m just wanting to do stuff...dont care what it is but i am doing it....i just sailed through christmas....at the island....and just had

A SISTER'S PROMISE

beautiful weather.....i love you and know how hard things are but you are funny, sexy, sweet and the world is yours go for it....big love your sister.....and april will be out of control...when you come....we will have a blast love me

## January 4ᵗʰ 2010 6:55 am I received a face book message from Mary

January 4, 2010 at 5:55am

HAPPY NEW YEAR JUDY!! 2010 is for travel & fun, fun, fun.

## January 5ᵗʰ 2010 I sent Cher a face book message

i got my passport!!!!! just got home from doing a zumba lesson with my girl friend from work and man did i sweat my butt off. it was sooo much fun. we are going to go every tuesday. i am doing my best to quit smoking. i'm getting in shape so i can walk the island!!!!!! i love you and i miss you. i'm so proud of you..... keep walking girl... can't keep us down!!!! love ya can't wait to come there.

A passport.!!!! One step closer to getting to panama. Hurray!!!!!!!

## January 18ᵗʰ, 2010 I sent a email to Cher

Sent: Monday, January 18, 2010 10:07 AM
Subject: judy

hey sis,
long time no hear from. doing ok here. was sick the last two days with the flew. feel a little better today. had all kinds of crap happen

of course, i'm on the edge anyway and for him to add to the stress is uncalled for. by the way mary told me to get the flight information from you to come to panama. i need to look up what the ticket is going to cost and try to arrange it all so i can inform work of when i need off. other than that it's the same old crap day after day. i went to the doctor and got on medication to get me back on the right track. i was really starting to get way too depressed and couldn't even think anymore. i'm going to zumba on tuesdays with friends from work so trying to get in shape. i love ya & miss you. write me back so i can look up the airlines. hope all is well. Love ya Judy

### Cher sent me a face book message that night

Sent: Monday, January 18, 2010 6:27 PM
Subject: Cher Hughes sent you a message on Face book...

Cher sent you a message.

"hey am really busy right now will write you soon all my love xoxoxo"

### ⁓⁓January 24th, 2010 12:48pm Mary wrote on my face book wall

Mary wrote on your timeline.
"Went to Alice's b'day party with Scott & Ronda. 50 is big..had a great time, she had a big crowd from work. Love, me"

### ⁓⁓January 27th, 2010 I received a face book message from cher

miss ya
everything great...hope you are well....and soon is your bday

# A SISTER'S PROMISE

## February 1st, 2010 I sent cher an email to Cher

Sent: Monday, February 1, 2010 7:09 PM
Subject: judy

hey sis,
sorry i haven't been on computer in a while. been crazy as usual. still working too many hours even worked 4 hours on saturday. i hope you are doing ok. i checked your face book looks like you're having a little bit of fun. i just don't understand why people have to be so damn mean. doug & i have been talking a lot more. we are still trying to be friends, he is falling apart. crying everyday and it is really sad that i almost feel sorry for him. i know what it's like and so do you. i am just trying to take one day at a time and see if i can make it thru. i really miss you and hope you know that i love you very much and i think about you all the time. hang in there sis
things have to get better. love ya judy

## February 1st, 2010 I received a face book message from cher

ready
hey go to in box and compose and click on to push c and my name will come up and send me a message....are you good.....love your sis

## February 14th, 2010 I sent a email to Cher

Sent: Sunday, February 14, 2010 12:17 PM
Subject: judy

hey sis,
well i did it. i went last tuesday and got 7 of my teeth pulled and i have 3 other appointments and then april 8th they pull the rest of my

top front and will leave 5 of my bottom teeth and put in dentures right then. WOW IT FRICKN HURTS. my mouth is so sore. i went tuesday at 5 pm and went back to work on wednesday and worked all week. i'm trying to save my time. i want to try and come the first week of may now since i'm having all this teeth shit done. i want to make sure i am healed and my teeth fit right so i can enjoy myself. if i go the week before my birthday then i will have to come back for the end of month hell at work. i would rather get that over with and know that i will come back to not so much of a headache. the damn dentist told my to take tylenol can you believe he did not prescribe anything for pain? i haven't smoked a cigarette since tuesday at 4:30. i hope i can quit for good. my mouth hurts so bad i don't even want to think about trying to smoke a cig. i am pretty excited about doing this for myself. i'm hoping it will be the incentive that i need to get the rest of me in shape. i still love going to my zumba classes. i want to look good when i come. the dentist said he hasn't seen teeth that bad in a while so he said it could have been effecting my vision and making me feel so sluggish. i know it will be worth it. well i gotta go for now. i'm going to rinse with salt water and try to stop the throbbing. love ya write back soon

## February 23rd, 2010 I received a face book message from Cher

Sent: Tuesday, February 23, 2010 10:57 PM
Subject: Cher Hughes wrote on your Wall…

"cant wait till you girls come here …weather great heard you were freezing….did you hear about our aunt….she is so much fun….hope you are well…..and mary is better…."

## February 25th, 2010 I sent an email to Cher with a picture of a nice boat

Sent: Thursday, February 25, 2010 7:39 PM
Subject: judy

Hey i found the boat you need . this is unreal. we would definitely have a great time on this. hope you are doing ok. love ya. Just something to wish about!

I sent the same picture of the boat to Mary

Sent: Thursday, February 25, 2010 7:46 PM
Subject: judy

Hey Mary,
how are you? i hope you are recovering. i found the boat that i told cher to get for when we go to the island. i've had to get my teeth pulled and i'm getting dentures so i'm hoping i will heal quick. I'm thinking we should go to cher's the first of may. if i go the week before my birthday i will have to come back to end of month crap at work and i'm hoping my mouth will not hurt.

are you feeling ok? i know you have to hurt. that sucks. are you going to be ok to travel now? well gotta go for now. just had to show you the boat we need to be one. just got home from work and need to get something to eat. oh boy more soup hurray for me!!!!!!!!!!!! love ya and hurry up and heal woman. lol love ya judy

## March 7th, 2010 Mary posted on Cher's face book wall

Hi = Thanks for surprise phone call! I am walking 1 mile a day to keep up, but can't push, pull, except to eat! This really stinks! Mary
March 7, 2010 at 2:22pm

## JUDY BARBER

### March 7, 2010 I received an email from Mary she had talked to Cher

Sent: Sunday, March 7, 2010 2:27 PM
Subject:
So how are you doing? What is the dentist got planned for you? I am still home & bored, all I seem to do is eat. Not a good thing.
Cher called to say hello, it is raining like crazy there, which means not much to do for her either.
Then when I am busy I complain too!! Love ya' Mary

### March 12th, 2010 11:43 a.m. Mary posted on my face book wall

"Hi There! How are you doing? What's new? Hope you are able to eat by now."

### March 19, 2010 I received my LAST email from Cher

Sent: Friday, March 19, 2010 5:52 PM
Subject: Fwd: Tr : Pictures of carnaval

hello i wanted you all to see that i am fine and hanging with the devils...ha ha this was carnival in bocas ..thought you might enjoy them....scroll down or view...love you all cher

## A SISTER'S PROMISE

We found out later that Cher had gone to a party with some friends at Wild Bills house. Everyone spent the night but the next day Bill asked Cher to stay behind because he wanted to talk to her about buying some of her property. This is when he took her life and changed my world forever.

## MARCH 20TH STRANGE POST ON CHER'S FACEBOOK PAGE

(WE LATER FOUND OUT THAT WILD BILL WAS POSTING THESE)
thankful
island flowers blue water
March 20, 2010 at 8:51pm

birthday zack brown band
I just discovered a daily photo
March 21, 2010 at 9:09pm

bill and janes party 2010 (THE SICK B WOULD POST PICS OF HIS PARTY)
I just discovered a daily photo
March 22, 2010 at 9:16pm

girls n bubba
I just discovered a daily photo
March 23, 2010 at 9:32pm

rocky horror and christmas parade
allie great kisser
March 25, 2010 at 9:31pm

florida 1990
I just discovered a daily photo
March 26, 2010 at 9:20pm

JUDY BARBER

Those same post repeated for days. We did not understand why Cher was
Posting these things but would not email anyone back.

## March 26th, 2010 a post on Cher's face book wall from Mark
CALL ME!
March 26, 2010 at 10:19pm

## March 30th, 2010 A post on Cher's face book wall from Sandi
Hey Cher, give me call . Sandi
March 30, 2010 at 8:45am

## APRIL 1ST 2010 I SENT AN EMAIL TO CHER AND MARY

Sent: Thursday, April 1, 2010 8:56 PM
Subject: judy

hey i'm looking at the flights to panama and continental has flights to houston then panama. is that the right flight, mary can you fly your airline.

cher what is the plane from panama to you?

i'm thinking of leaving may 2 (since end of month i work late and maybe have to work a few hours on saturday) so leave on sunday may 2 and return on may 15 which would be 12 days in panama and 2 days of travel.

i need to know if that will work for everybody.. i'm ready to book it how bout you mary?

**A SISTER'S PROMISE**

I CAN'T WAIT, I'M GETTING SOOOOOOOOOOOO EXCITED.

email me back and i will get on computer tomorrow. this is not an april fool joke either. LOL HAHA i'm ready to complete the plan and know that i'm really going.

love ya guys,

email me back asap.
love judy


Sent: Thursday, April 1, 2010 9:01 PM
Subject: Re: what's up?

hey there i just went today back to dentist and did a fitting for my teeth. i go next thursday april 8th to get it all done. this is it!!!!!!!!!!!!!!!! i'm scared & excited. i've healed up a lot but i know it's gonna hurt like heck again. but it will all be worth it. i just sent you gals an email about vacation. i'll be all good to travel i'm sure. glad to hear your getting better mary. IT'S TIME TO GET AWAY AND PLAY. email me back. i promise i'll be on computer tomorrow night. love ya's

## April 2nd, 2010 I emailed Mary and Cher

Sent: Friday, April 2, 2010 7:18 PM
Subject: Re: judy

hi mary,
i have my time approved at work, i looked at tickets and this one looks good. cher can you tell us what the other airport is that we should fly into. i would rather get to panama during the day then try to get there at night if i am going to meet you mary. what flight are you

## JUDY BARBER

thinking about? i can fly back by myself it's straight thru so no problem. I'M READY NOW. HURRAY i want to for sure get this booked this weekend. SO CHER EMAIL US BACK. mary let me know what your flight would be. love yas

### April 3rd, 2010 I received an email from Mary

Date: Saturday, April 3, 2010, 3:06 AM

Hi Judy,
It is too difficult for me to fly thru Miami our flights are always full going there. I will fly Houston/Panama City (PTY) arriving about 1pm. If you go on American, we can meet at the airport, take a cab to the hotel, catch our next flight next morning. The reason we have done this in the past is that we couldn't make it across the whole city to catch the last flight to Bocas. I assume it is still the same.

Greg & Becky are in Honolulu right now, I am ready for some island life too! I suggest a swimsuit, some cotton tee shirts & sneakers, it is hot and no need to dress up. Don't pack any liquid more that 3 ounces—including make up, perfume, tooth paste or deodorant, I carry a few .99 travel size from Target. Also just carry enough to put in a small suitcase carry on so there is no chance of lost bags. Will advise anything else as I think of it. Here we go!!! Mary

### April 4th, 2010 I emailed Mary

Sent: Sunday, April 4, 2010 7:17 PM
Subject: Re: judy
hi mary,
i just booked the flight. WOW I'M SOOOOOOOO EXCITED. i went to beach today for a few hours to try and get a little sun at a time. i sure

don't want to burn. i even bought new pajamas today. I'M GOING ALL OUT!!!!! i had to say farewell to the ones i had for eight years. lol can't wait to see you and cher,. i could use some girl time., love ya's cher email us the flight info so i can book that too. HERE WE GO IS RIGHT

I booked my flight on April 4$^{th}$ 2010. Wow what a birthday present to myself and I felt I deserved it. I wanted to celebrate my birthday with Cher which was April 26$^{th}$ but due to work I waited until after month end rush. I was leaving for Bocas del Toro May 2, 2010 and returning May 15 and Mary would be meeting me there. I was so excited that I had my flight and was finally going to panama after 10 years of Cher telling me how beautiful it was. What I did not know was that Cher had already been murdered.

### Mary emailed me back

Sent: Sunday, April 4, 2010 8:35 PM
Subject: Re: judy

I am so proud of you!! You are a can do chic!!! Mary

## April 7$^{th}$, 2010 a post on Cher's face book wall from Mark

WTF are you!
April 7, 2010 at 10:24pm

## April 10$^{th}$ 2010 a post on Cher's face book wall from Susie

Hi Cher... Was thinking of you and haven't seen your around or heard from you in a while....
April 10, 2010 at 1:39pm

## JUDY BARBER

### ～April 13th, 2010 I sent an email to Cher

Sent: Tuesday, April 13, 2010 7:19 PM
Subject: judy

hey email me. i'm worried about you. no one has heard from you. dad is in a panic. call & let us know you are ok. i have bought my ticket so i need to know you are there. love ya judy

### ～April 13th, 2010 7:29pm I posted this message on Cher's face book wall

Judy wrote on Cher Hughes's Wall.
"cher please call me. no one has heard from you in a while. dad is trying to get in touch with you too. i love you & miss you love your sis judy"

### ～April 14th, 2010 received face book from Mary

Hi Judy, No one has heard from Cher, including you Dad, who is calling Grandma to hear what's new. I just got msg from Mark in Bocas, was in ctc with her daily, said she left msg she was going sailing. My guess they are out of satelight range. I will adv Grandma & she can call your Dad. It is easy to lose a phone or computer down there, but let me know if you hear back from her or John. Hope you are feeling better & ready to smile the whole time on our big adventure! We will need to make a new drink!!!

### ～April 14th, 2010 received face book message

James
Message from Aunt Mary

Judy,
Mary spoke with Henry. Apparently Cher is sailing with friends. Probably much ado about nothing. Mary is asking everyone to contact her (rather than Grandma) so no one will get confused.
Uncle Jim

### April 14th, 2010 received a face book from Scott

Have you heard from Cher lately.
I spoke to Mary and we were wondering?

### April 15th, 2010 Mary posted on Cher's face book wall

Cher—Hey you!!! Hear you are on a sailboat having a blast!! You are in big trouble for worrying us back here living the boring life. PLEASE text or contact somebody soon!! We hope to see you soon & also enjoy a sail. LOVE YOU!! See ya next month. Mary
April 15, 2010 at 5:08pm

### April 15th, 2010 6:58 p.m. Mary posted on my face book wall

"well the only layover i'm looking forward to is the one we have in panama. dad & gram had been calling me to see if i had heard from cher. i guess she is sailing which is a great thing. i can't wait to go. i'm soo excited."

### April 15th, 2010 I sent a face book message back to Mary

thanks. i feel a lot better knowing that. dad & grandma where calling to see if i had heard from her and i hadn't which was very odd. glad to know she's ok.

## JUDY BARBER

### Mary emailed me back

Date: Thursday, April 15, 2010, 11:00 PM

Hi Judy,
I am trying to find Cher. I have ctc'd her face book friends to see what they know. Mark got a text from her saying she was going sailing—which means probably out of range for cell or computer. Or she lost/broken either or both, easy to do way out there.

Dave replied that he heard she sold out & left. Selling the rental would be a good thing & I know she had serious lookers not long ago. Left on a sail maybe—but I want more info. Saw your msg to her, so when I know something you will know something & you ctc me with any news.

I called your Dad & Grandma & told them that is what I heard & not to worry as she does have reliable friends who have her back.

I left a msg on John's phone to call me if he knows anything, I think I should be touchstone for information, as Dad & Gram are easily shaken & don't get the story straight anymore, so lets keep things simple.

I believe we need to keep this information confidential, so use email & NOT FACEBOOK (just hi, call me stuff there).

She is probably basking in the sun & will be back soon and we will scold her soundly when we see her.

I am in London an extra day due to volcano, will be back in states on Saturday afternoon—I may go straight to St. Louis & check on things there. Love, Mary

## April 17th, 2010 Alice posted on Cher's face book wall

Geez girl, you gotta keep people informed when you're gonna be gone for several days. Hope you're having fun!
April 16, 2010 at 7:03pm

## April 17th, 2010 I received a face book message from Mary

April 17, 2010 at 7:27am
Hi Judy! Am so glad Cher mystery is solved! Am still looking forward to our getaway. Do you like to sail?

## April 19th, 2010 Mary posted on Cher's face book wall

CALL OR EMAIL somebody soon. I am stuck in London waiting for skies to clear of volcano ash. I spoke w/your Dad just before I left & he needs to talk to you. Mary
April 19, 2010 at 1:46am

## April 20th, 2010 sent face book to Scott
Hi Scott,
i haven't heard from her. i have been emailing her but not sure what is going on. if i hear anything i will let you know.

### Scott sent me a message back

Will continue to try to find her

## JUDY BARBER

### I sent an email to Mary that same evening

Sent: Tuesday, April 20, 2010 6:46 PM
Subject: Re: Cher

Hi Mary,
i have not heard from cher at all. grandma just called again today and left a message around 11:00 on my house phone, she said my dad is about ready to have a heart attack. cher should really let people know what's going on. i will let you know if i hear from her.
love ya

p.s. thanks for the birthday card. i laughed my butt off.

### April 21st, 2010 Mary received a face book message from Susie

Date: Wed, Apr 21, 2010 at 12:58 AM
Subject: Susie sent you a message on Face book...
To: Mary W
Re: Cher?
Mary, I was told for you to contact John, he is the one that knows the details... I have not been in contact with him and do not know how to contact him... Keep me posted, and good luck... S

### April 21st, 2010 I received an email from Mary

Date: Wednesday, April 21, 2010, 1:18 PM

Hi Judy,

HAPPY BIRTHDAY!!!!

Please know that I have 3 face book returns from Bocas—they all say Cher has sold everything, they know who she sold to, he is taking care of her dogs til she gets back. NOT COOL to not call anyone.

I am in London & they are letting us have some free phone time, so I will call your Dad & tell him the same.even though sailing for 5 weeks now is stretching it—I DO HOPE she is ok.

I hope to be home in a day or 2, this is getting old.
Love, Mary

### I emailed Mary back

Sent: Wednesday, April 21, 2010 6:50 PM
Subject: Re: Cher

WHAT? how could she sell everything when we are coming down? i don't believe she wouldn't tell us. keep me posted. Love Judy

### I sent an email to Cher

Sent: Wednesday, April 21, 2010 6:55 PM
Subject: judy

Cher,
what the heck is going on? i already have a flight reserved to come and see you on may 2nd and stay until the 15th. please email me and let me know you are ok. everyone is saying you have sold everything. i don't believe that.

i'm worried about you. PLEASE CALL OR EMAIL ME ASAP.
love judy

JUDY BARBER

## April 22nd, 2010 I received an email from Mary

Date: Thursday, April 22, 2010, 6:56 AM

I know, am worried as even on a sail ship they should have been to port by now. Did you hear she got an apt in Panama City? Even thought she sold the island, maybe she made arrangements to stay for a few weeks when we get there—her dogs and things are still there. John tried to talk her out of this, so that is another confirmation. We shall see......Mary

### I emailed Mary back

Sent: Thursday, April 22, 2010 8:45 PM
Subject: Re: Cher

she told me she was looking at a condo in panama on the 26th floor and it was all made of marble but she made it sound like she was going to sell the apts in bocas and invest in the apt in panama. she told me she would never sell that island. i will let you know if i hear from her. this is really strange for her not to call for this long. love ya

## April 23rd, 2010 I received an email from Mary

Sent: Friday, April 23, 2010 5:53 AM
Subject: Re: Cher
I am home now. Nothing new to report.

## April 24th, 2010 Alice posted on Cher's face book wall

Cher—We're all very worried about you. Please call someone so we

know you're alright. We don't have any way of knowing if it's you posting to your wall so only a phone call is gonna cover this. CALL ASAP
April 24, 2010 at 8:19pm

## April 25th 2010 I sent a face book message to Cher

cher please call me or someone. i am supposed to be leaving on the 2nd to come & see you.

### I received an email from Mary

Sent: Sunday, April 25, 2010 9:28 AM
Subject: Re: Cher

Hi Judy,

Well, what should we do? What is the latest news? What dates are your tickets? Mary

### I emailed Mary back

Sent: Sunday, April 25, 2010 10:39 AM
Subject: Re: Cher

i haven't heard anything either. my ticket is for may 2nd a week from today and i return on the 15th.. i don't know what we will do once we get there if we don't get in touch with cher. i don't have the money for a motel for 2 weeks. i'm really confused as to what is happening with cher.

### JUDY BARBER

## I received another email from Mary

Sent: Sunday, April 25, 2010 11:47 AM
Subject: Re: Cher

Hi—
Your Dad Just called me. He has no news & wants to know what we are doing.

He gave me John's email. I am going to email John & see if we can stay with him. Is that ok with you? You can see his house from Cher's house on the island. I know John from childhood, but want your input. Mary

## Mary copied me on an email she sent to friend of our Family in Bocas

Sent: Sunday, April 25, 2010 12:09 PM mary wrote:
Subject: Trip to Bocas

Hi John,

We are very concerned not hearing from Cher. Please advise what you know. I have contacted her face book friends down there & they all agree that she sold & went on a sailboat—just spoke with Henry & he said he learned same from you. Do you know who & where she went?

She was really looking forward to us coming, so this is not good.

Does she still own any property where we can stay? Can we stay with you if we don't hear from Cher? Are her apartment all rented on Bocas, could we stay there?

# A SISTER'S PROMISE

Well Judy & I are supposed to leave for Panama City on May 2. She is on American Airlines & I am on Continental Air. Usually I stay at the Marriott in Panama City for 1 nght, then fly to Bocas the next day. We have not yet bought tckts to Bocas.

Sorry you are the one there, so I need to ask you = What should we do?

Mary

## This is the email Mary received back

On Sun, Apr 25, 2010 at 2:18 PM, John wrote:

you know what i know last tex from her was march 30...going sailing N WEST CST S amer.. well call when i get back... cher sold all property ... you are welcome to stay with me... man that bought apts.. renting by month now... i think they are full... bill is out of country at this time.. do not know who she left with.. that is what concerns me.. she was very depressed...


On Sun, Apr 25, 2010 at 3:23 PM, mary wrote:
Subject: Re: Trip to Bocas
To: John

Thanks John!

Are you in Panama now? Will you be in Bocase May 3?

So much for our vacation, looks like we are on a hunt for Cher. Mary

JUDY BARBER

### John's response

On Sun, Apr 25, 2010 at 2:31 PM, John wrote:
i will try to find out where her things are in panama city... i think she was staying with some gay guys..when she was last heard from...

### Mary's response to John
From: mary
Date: Sun, Apr 25, 2010 at 2:38 PM
Subject: Re: Trip to Bocas
To: John

Thanks, great to know you will be there when we arrive. Judy has purchased tkt to arrive Panama City on May 2 & return 15th. I am standyby on Continental, so my dates are flexible but will of course stay with Judy. Mary

### John's response

On Sun, Apr 25, 2010 at 2:50 PM, John wrote:
can pick you up in bocas ...you can only get am flights as air port is closed in pm for repairs....i will try to get you some leads to ck on in panama city... like i said your welcome to stay here but i have to leave on may 11 then stay nite panama city .. i have closeing on realastate fri may 14.... but could always go to panama city early are..few days.. just let me know... man that bought all cher property lives out here by me... he ship all her personal things to panama city...will try to find out more..

### Mary's response

On Sun, Apr 25, 2010 at 3:55 PM, mary wrote:

Great—so as of now, you will pick us up in Bocas on the 3rd. We will make those flight arrangements a little later in case there is something we should do in Panama sooner, if you get an address in Panama.

Keep me posted with any news.

I will call Henry.

Mary

### John's response

On Sun, Apr 25, 2010 at 3:11 PM, John wrote:
yes i have call in to Dave he knows where that place is and mabe phone # when you book return flights bocas to panama city we can all go on am flight may 11 i have some one to take as to bocas in my boat.. i also have other girl that was staying with cher in panama city at guy condo.. says she knows nothing.. i think she is lying she was there with cher for two weeks.. just got off phone with Dave he has no # for jim in panama city .. as he called him guy .. Dave said he deleted # long time ago.. but says he will talk with girl in bacas..

### Mary's response

From: mary
Date: Sun, Apr 25, 2010 at 3:19 PM
Subject: Re: Trip to Bocas
To: John

Good, we are getting a few more pieces to this puzzle. Mary

JUDY BARBER

### John's response

On Sun, Apr 25, 2010 at 3:30 PM, John wrote:
out of here for now need to shut off power plant.... will ck emailin mornings around 7 to 8 if you need any thing...

### Mary emailed me

Sent: Sunday, April 25, 2010 3:02 PM Subject: Re: Cher
i wouldnit mind staying with John but when do you leave to go back to work? John hasnit heard from cher either?

### Mary emailed me again

Sent: Sunday, April 25, 2010 3:10 PM
Subject: Re: Cher

John has heard nothing from Cher. As I understand it, there is a girl who was supposed to go sailing also & then decided not to go. John spoke with her but John didn't believe her. This I got from your Dad, and am not sure what it means.

I have a trip on the 8th, but will trade it as soon as able. I plan on coming back with you on the 15t Mary

### I was copied on an email that Scott sent to Mary

From: Scott
To: Mary
Sent: Sunday, April 25, 2010 6:10 PM
Subject: RE: Trip to Bocas

what Bank does she deal with concerning the sale of the property, What was the lawyer or closing co that transferred funds etc.

I am thinking that may be a way to track her down via money and spending.

I am now really worried. now and I think we need to contact authorities soon.
I would hate to wait and the regret it.
Scott

## APRIL 26th 2010….. MY BIRTHDAY AND NO EMAIL FROM CHER

From: Continental Airlines, Inc.
Date: Mon, Apr 26, 2010 at 8:03 AM
Subject: ePass Itinerary and Receipt
To: MARY

Mary has purchased her ticket to Panama

## April 26th, 2010 Mary contacts John

On Mon, Apr 26, 2010 at 8:36 AM, mary wrote:
Hi again,
Only other thing I can think of is where is the money? Did she put it in the bank, did she purchase anything big, any unusual withdrawls from account.

Did she bank in Bocas or Panama?

Please let me know if there is anything we can check in Panama

## JUDY BARBER

before we come to Bocas. When is latest I should book Panama/Bocas flights?

Any other ideas? Mary

### John's response

On Mon, Apr 26, 2010 at 9:25 AM, John wrote:
same bank in bocas and panama deal was done by attorneys ... i dont know how it all went ...you will need talk to her attorney i will try to find out who it is.. as i dont know... i hope she put monies in bank.. bill told me when he shipped her personal things there was over 9000.oo cash he sent... plus jewelry...i have not talked to here before all was done..

On Mon, Apr 26, 2010 at 8:33 AM, John wrote:
have you been to david city in panama ... you could fly there from panama city.. i could meet you there..i could drive cher van there we could drive back across country to my place...i think her attorney is in david... you would fly to david but back to panamacity from bocas.. same price..

From: mary
Date: Mon, Apr 26, 2010 at 8:50 AM
Subject: Re: Trip to Bocas
To: John

Yes, have been to David, and as we would come in Monday morning, maybe we could meet with her attorney that day.

I just made hotel reservations 2May/3May in Panama.

# A SISTER'S PROMISE

Hard to believe Cher would let someone near that kind of money!!

### A post on Cher's face book wall from her girlfriend Lindsey

WTFRU WOMAN?????
April 26, 2010 at 11:42am

### ⁓⁓⁓April 27th, 2010 I received an email from Mary

Sent: Tuesday, April 27, 2010 8:22 AM
Subject: Cher

Judy—
I just facebooked same msg to 4 people on Cher's face book from Bocas—they have all left msgs on her wall looking for her—I have been in ctc with then these last few weeks,
Mark, Susie, Sandi , Dave.

I said "Judy & I are arriving next week. We are staying with John, we may want to meet with Cher's friends & gather info—will advise when we arrive. Have you heard anything new?"

I told Dave " I know I can depend on you, I am really scared, pls let me/ John know anything you have heard."

I think we need to keep everyone as our friend, but keep all information we get to ourselves. John will be a big help, but I am not sure what we are looking at. As you saw, he said she was depressed, drinking & drugs. I promised to tell only you.

I have been hoping she will ctc us even yet, but this is not good. Are you ok with what we need to do? I hate that your big vacation is turning sinister.

## JUDY BARBER

Any ideas what else we can do before Sunday? Oh, we need to book flights from Panama to David/Bocas. Do you mind if I book us both just to simplify things? I need your passport number & exact birthdate to do that.

Mary

### Mary copied me on an email she sent to Cher

Date: Tue, Apr 27, 2010 at 12:06 PM
Subject: coming to Bocas
To: cher hughes

Cher—

Judy & I leave on Sunday to come to Panama. We will be in the Marriott on Sunday night. We are buying tickets to fly to David on Monday morning, John is going to pick us up, and we are staying at his place.

We know you sold everything to Bill, left town without paying commission to Jim, the realtor from DC Realty.

I have facebooked with Mark, Susie, Sandi, & Dave. No one knows where you are.

Your Dad is frantic, he has called me, Gram, John, Dave.

PLEASE CONTACT SOMEONE—If you are ok, but out of reach, that is fine, but let us know so we don't chase our tails & spend money & time for nothing.
WE WILL FIND YOU!! WE LOVE YOU!!! Mary

## April 28th, 2010 Mary copied me on email she sent to John

Date: Wed, Apr 28, 2010 at 7:58 AM
Subject: Bocas
To: John

Hi John,

Scott called Jim the realtor, who also confirmed Cher is gone, that other people are also looking for her. Jim said she is absolutely not in Bocas. Scott was going to try & call Bill to see if he would say where he shipped Cher's stuff.
We are having second thoughts about coming to Bocas, hate to spend money on flights knowing Cher isn't there. Do you think we should call the police? Hate to do that if she is in trouble with the police already.

Do you have anymore leads? Do you have any suggestions?

Mary


## I received an email from Mary

Sent: Wednesday, April 28, 2010 2:07 PM
Subject: Fwd: Bocas

I just spoke with American Embassy in Panama. I gave Cher's info, they will check hospitals & jails.
They wanted her email even though I said there was no communication for 5 weeks, they need to first try & connect her, make sure she wants us to know where she is. My contact is Sally, assistant to L F., Consul General—she seemed competant, hope to get email from her soon.

## JUDY BARBER

I gave this info to Henry. He seems to want Judy & I to go to Bocas/David to try & speak with attorney, bank, friends, even though we are all in agreement she is not there. Judy & I are thinking it over.

Scott—Bill Sanches who now owns island & shipped Cher's stuff is in Mexico on vacation with his wife. So we need to get shipping address from him when he returns.

Mary

### April 28th, 2010 Mary emailed John and me

Date: Wed, Apr 28, 2010 at 7:06 PM
Subject: Re: Fwd: Bocas

Hi,

John, can you get address in Panama from Bill?
I don't have capacity to text, email is my best bet. Thx.
What Number to check entry to country? Do you have her passport number? Henry didn't have that earlier today.

Judy, I have Cher's social sec #, birthdate & last FL drivers license number. Do you have your birth certificate and anything that proves you are her sister? We may need to prove relationship.

US Embassy didn't ask for identification from me....as yet.

Mary

### I emailed Mary back

## A SISTER'S PROMISE

On Wed, Apr 28, 2010 at 8:17 PM, Judy wrote:
i also am bringing a promisory note that cher & i signed when she was here for the repairs she did on the house. i want to compare her signature to the one on the docs for the sale of the property or her condo. i don't know what the heck to believe. WOW

## April 28th 2010 received another email from Mary

Date: Wednesday, April 28, 2010, 8:17 PM

YOU WON'T BELIEVE THIS!!!

Just now received face book msg from SAMANTHA, woman in Bocas. She says she just spoke with someone in contact with Cher—she is just upset & needs a break, I should chill.

I about had a sht fit!!!

I replied at this point I need PROOF OF LIFE—who was this contact & when & where did they see Cher.

Mary

### HOW I WISH THAT WAS TRUE

#### I emailed Mary back

On Wed, Apr 28, 2010 at 8:52 PM

i am not going to believe anything until i hear it from cher. i don't know who these people are but i know cher would have at least called dad by now. this is getting crazier by the minute.

🙰 JUDY BARBER

## I sent an email to John, Scott and Mary

From: judy
To: John ; Scott ; mary
Sent: Wednesday, April 28, 2010 9:15 PM
Subject: Re: Fwd: Fwd: Bocas

i have my birth cert and jen just sent some pictures to her work of me and cher together and is going to print them out in color tomorrow. i asked Alice tonight is she could get a copy of chers birth cert and ss card and passport. dad should have this. Alice said she did but she has to find it. i gave her Johns email as well in case she finds it after we are gone

## Mary emailed me back

From: mary
Sent: Wednesday, April 28, 2010 9:24 PM
Subject: Re: Fwd: Bocas

Yeah, if you can shit kick someone over face book, I just did.

TELL ME TO CHILL!!!, Cher has her phone # & she will call if she needs anything She told me to maybe contact John.

My reply was"I am in contact with John. WHO ARE YOU IN CONTACT WITH?"

She hasnt' answered. I believe she is full of crap & just wants to be in on things, but don't screw with us at this point. But, I still want names.

Good ideas you have.....this is still a work in progress. Mary

## April 28th, 2010 received email from mary

From: mary w
To: Judy
Cc: John ; Scott
Sent: Wednesday, April 28, 2010 9:55 PM
Subject: Re: Fwd: Bocas

I agree. Hope to get address in Panama where her stuff was shipped. That is where we will go on Monday. Then we will visit the Embassy. Unless we get more info. OK?

## APRIL 29th, 2010 received email from Scott

From: Scott
To: Mary ; John; judy
Sent: Thursday, April 29, 2010 10:41 AM
Subject: RE: Bocas

That is still not any thing close to a direct contact.
she said, she heard from "someone" , who knows cher.
that is not a direct line.
who did she talk to, name , number etc etc.
Scott

## APRIL 29TH, 2010 Mary copied me on email to John

From: mary
To: John ; Judy ; Scott
Sent: Thursday, April 29, 2010 9:28 PM
Subject: Cher's Lawyer

## JUDY BARBER

Hi again John,

Please advise who Cher's lawyers are.

We want to ask them to give Cher a message from us to contact anyone in the family immediately.

We think she is at least in contact with her lawyers.

Thanks, Mary

---

Mary and I had talked on the phone and decided it would not be good to go
to Bocas if Cher is not there. Mary knew how much I was looking forward
to going on vacation so she suggested we get away and go to Las Vegas for three days. At this point we had no idea where Cher was nor did we know where
to look if we went to Panama. Las Vegas sounded like a great idea. Mary
also invited my sister Alice to go as well.

## APRIL 30th, 2010 Mary copied me on email to John

From: mary
To: John ; Judy ; Scott
Sent: Friday, April 30, 2010 1:45 AM
Subject: Latest Plan

Hi again John!

Well after all these emails, phone calls, face book. I am exhausted.
I believe Cher is not in Bocas, she is probably in Panama City or out

## A SISTER'S PROMISE

on a boat. If she doesn't want to be contacted, no use coming. If she is in trouble, we can't walk the country looking for her.

I have made a missing person report with the US Embassy in Panama City. I hope she contacts someone before they contact me.

I have called Henry and explained all this to him. He is still very worried, but after speaking with Bill I feel we have reached a brick wall. Judy & I have been planning a vacation for almost a year. We have decided to cancel flights to Panama and go to Las Vegas for 3 nights.

John, we are all so grateful for all your information, your gracious offer to let us stay with you, to pick us up from airports. Mostly we are glad you are Cher's friend, we know she makes her own decisions—even the really bad ones. So, thanks again for all you did and all you offered to do, it made all this craziness easier.

### April 30th, 2010 Mary sent me my airline confirmation:

From: mary
To: Judy
Sent: Friday, April 30, 2010 9:01 AM
Subject: Fwd: JUDY B TAMPA 01MAY10

## MAY 1ST WENT TO VEGAS WITH MARY AND ALICE

Your lodging Details

LITTLE Hotel And Casino

Address:
Xxx Las Vegas Boulevard South, Las Vegas, NV, US, xxx Get Directions

## JUDY BARBER

A marvel of modern architecture Little great onyx-hued pyramid has become the most distinctive landmark on the Las Vegas Strip. Conveniently located at the southern end of the world-famous Las Vegas Strip, the Little is adjacent to Marks Baily and the Extra. Complimentary trams are available for transportation between all three properties.

Check In:      May 01, 2010 15:00    Nights: 3
Check Out:    May 04, 2010 11:00    Room Type:    Deluxe

I had never been to Las Vegas and we had a really nice time. It was a great distraction from all the worrying about Cher. We did talk about where she could be or what may have happened. We just assumed that Cher was out of touch and would be in contact with us as soon as she was able. We also said that when she did contact us we were sure going to let her have it for worrying us the way she has.

### May 2nd, 2010 a post on Cher's face book wall from Brenda

CALL SOMEBODY! PLEASE
May 2, 2010 at 3:49pm

### May 4th, 2010 we left Las Vegas

Since I had already taken the time off work to go on vacation. I flew to St. Louis with my sister and stayed with her until May 15th. I visited family and just hung around and relaxed. I needed the break.

### May 15th, 2010 I flew back to Florida

I left St. Louis at 11:25pm and arrived back in Florida at 4:52 pm. My husband and daughter picked me up at the airport. I was happy to be back home and had to get myself ready to go back to work. I did not have the story of Panama to tell my coworkers but was grateful that I did get away.

## May 17th, 2010 I sent an email to Mary and Alice

Sent: Monday, May 17, 2010 7:57 PM
Subject: judy

judy wanted to say a quick hello and thanks again for the vacation. i'm back at work in my new position that sucks but work is work. everything else going ok. miss you gals already.

love ya
Judy

## May 24th, 2010 I sent an email to Mary and Alice

Sent: Monday, May 24, 2010 10:14 PM
Subject: judy

hey everyone,
just wanted to keep everyone updated. i got a phone call today from my girl friend roxanne that i worked with for two different company with a vp named matt well matt called roxanne and said he has a position for her & i. he has the business set up like the first place we worked and her and i were managers. i've left him a message so i will probably talk to him tomorrow. i would love to work for him again. i really hate my new position so it really is perfect timing. jennifer moved in with her boyfriend friday. so

things are definitely changing around here. doug has some side jobs he is doing in the shed but we worked on the house over the weekend and didn't fight. LOL well i need to get ready for tomorrow. i love you all and thanks again for wonderful family time. i truly enjoyed it. love judy

## May 25th, 2010 I sent my resume for my new job

Sent: Tuesday, May 25, 2010 8:01 PM
Subject: judy's resume

Hey Matt,
attached is my resume. hope to hear from you soon.

thanks i really appreciate you considering me. Judy

## May 27th. 2010 Mary sent email to Embassy

From: mary
Date: Thu, May 27, 2010 at 12:38 PM
Subject: Cher Hughes
To: ACS@state.gov

Sally,

I am updating information I sent you April 29 & May 5 re: disappearance of Cher Hughes.

Things seem very dire. Still no word even to her sick father.

What I now know: She is not divorced from Dave H.. She has 2 bank accounts—1. N Bank in Bocas used for small local bills. 2. Gl Bank in Panama City for large monetary deposits. Dave is not on either account, maybe her father is.

Can your office see if there has been any activity with her ATM, or any transactions, where they transpired?

The last I can trace back on her activities is to Bill Cortez. I understand Bill Cortez is involved with land transactions in Bocas, his phone is xxx or xxx. He told me he purchased all her property in a cash transaction (rumor has it .50 on the $1.00 so about $600,000.00?).

—He said he can't advise the attorney, the amount, or any details because he signed a confidentiality statement. He said after the transaction, she called him from Panama City and requested he ship her remaining personal effects—including a large sum of cash & jewelry. (This is VERY suspect, Cher is very cautious with money—greedy and almost paranoid that someone would steal from her). She left her dogs—1 she has had for 11 years!!

Dave, her husband, his emails is XXXXX@gmail.com, Panama phone # 507-XXXX-XXXX
has made a police report with officer Brian in Bocas—I don't have much confidence in this.
Henry her father, his email is XXXXX@aol.com, USA phone # XXX-XXX-XXXX, has made a report with the FBI—I do not know if they have any jurisdiction in Panama.

PLEASE ADVISE!!! What else can we do? Can you check out the money trail, as I believe there lies the answer.

Do you have people who investigate this kind of thing? What is your involvment and procedures?

Thank you again, Mary

## JUDY BARBER

### ⁓May 28th Mary received email back from Embassy

From: Panama, ACS <Panama-ACS@state.gov>
Date: Fri, May 28, 2010 at 4:40 PM
Subject: RE: Cher Hughes
To: mary

Good Morning Mary
Thank you for your e-mail. We have been in contact with offices of the Government of Panama regarding the welfare and whereabouts of Cher Hughes, but we are still waiting for their responses. Sometimes, it could takes time. I would like to remind you that the Privacy Act prevents me to disclose information on Ms. Hughes without her authorization. Thank you.

Best Regards,
CF
American Citizens Services Unit
Unidad de Asistencia a Ciudadanos Estadounidenses
Consular Section / Sección Consular
U.S. Embassy Panama / Embajada de los Estados Unidos de América en Panamá

### ⁓May 29th received email from Mary

From: mary
To: Henry; Scott ; Judy
Sent: Saturday, May 29, 2010 1:04 PM
Subject: Fwd: Cher Hughes

Hi—

I have not responded to this email. The Privacy Act means they need to keep her information from me.

I am in London and can't figure what to do next. What do you guys think?

Mary

## May 31st, 2010 I received an email from mary

Date: Monday, May 31, 2010, 3:07 PM

Hey!
Been thinking about you…how did meeting re: new job go?
What's new with the house?

I am between trips, then 2 days off, may go to St. Louis and check up on Grandma then. Her car was broken into and she has to pay $500. deductible to get it fixed. I hate to see her spend the money, and I really hate the thought of her out driving around. That car still runs good even without a/c—can't replace it for $500.00.

Still worried about Cher. Since our trip Dave has called me twice, NOW he is worried about Cher. He thought she was just on a bender & would show eventually. Now he is worried about this Bill Cortez who bought the island. Bill Cortez just emailed me looking for John. I hope John stops to see Henry while in Missouri, maybe he will be more forthcoming with your Dad. I know we will eventually find the truth to this mess, just hope it will be soon.

Everyone got a big kick out of our video—was that just a month ago?!!!

Love, Mary

## JUDY BARBER

### June 1st, 2010 I started my new job.

I am now working for the same boss Matt that I had worked for when Cher moved to Panama years before. He actually sent me home from work the day she moved because I was so emotional. He understood how close I was to Cher and how much I missed her. I really did not realize how significant this would be.
I had his support when she moved and would have his support again once I found out Cher had been murdered. What are the odds?

### June 1st a post on Cher's face book wall from Chris
Cher, where are you ????
June 1, 2010 at 5:58pm

### June 6th, 2010 I sent an email to Mary

Sent: Sunday, June 6, 2010 3:11 PM
Subject: Re: what's new?

Hey Mary,
things are crazy as usual. new job is going ok i only got to train with the girl i'm replacing for a day and a half so monday should be really interesting. it's just gonna take me some time to get used to new computer systems etc. jen had to take doug to emergency room on wednesday he was so fricking sick. i picked him up in sarasota hospital after i got off work. then thursday jennifer went to her doctor and he sent her right to the emergency room cause she was running a fever and they thought she might have in infection that is making her breast swell up. well turns out its her thyroid. she still has to go to doctor to get mamagram for her breast. it's never ending here. as far as the house i have actually got the drywall up & mudded in kitchen so i'll be putting my cabinets back up this week. only have about 8

or 9 sheet left to put up. so i'm getting there. i still haven't heard from cher i have no idea whats going on there. keep me posted. still laughing about the trip to vegas. thanks again hope we can do it again. love ya gotta get back to drywall.

## June 6th, 2010 a post on Cher's face book wall from Alice

Cher, please contact a family memeber we're very worried about you. Have also contacted authorities to find you and we won't stop until we hear from you and only you.
June 6, 2010 at 8:53pm

## June 7th, 2010 I received face book message from Cher's Godmother

June 7, 2010 at 1:40am
Subject: Regarding Cher
Hi Judy, I am wondering if u have heard anything about Cher? Are the investigators still looking for her, or found out anything? Please email whatever you know as of now. Hope all is well with you. Thanks hon

## June 8th 2010 I sent a message back

Sent: Tuesday, June 8, 2010 7:39 PM
Subject: Re: Anne sent you a message on Face book...

Hi,
no we have not heard anything from her. latest is my aunt mary said my dad has contacted congressman, Dave supposedly has now filed a police report. i have no idea what has happened, i will keep you posted. love ya's judy

## JUDY BARBER

### June 8th, 2010 7:45pm I posted a face book message to everyone

Judy updated her status.
"hey everyone. been kinda crazy as usual. started new job on tuesday. doug in emergency room on wednesday then jennifer had t go to emergency room on thursday. trying not to be stressed. job going ok. lots to learn. been out of the loop for a while with processing but i will get it. hope everyone is doing well. miss everyone"

### June 11th, 2010 I received an email from Alice

Sent: Friday, June 11, 2010 8:36 PM
Subject: question for you

Mary needs to know when was the last email you got from Cher and do you still have it.

### June 13th, 2010 a post on Cher's face book page from Alice

Anyone—Please help. I would like to know when the last time anyone saw her, I'm trying to put together a timeline.
June 13, 2010 at 12:18pm ·

Alice Thank you for whatever you can do. I miss her very much and our dad is making himself sick with worry. If you find her or talk to her, please make sure she calls her dad.
June 23, 2010 at 9:58pm
Alice fyi—I am Cher's sister
June 23, 2010 at 10:05pm

### June 17th, 2010 Mary sent out an email to Family

Sent: Thursday, June 17, 2010 5:24 PM
Subject: Authorities re:Cher

Well today I got a phone call from the US Embassy, a phone call from Congressman's office. They also called Henry. The good news is, this case is upfront and serious!!

I also got an email from the local Embassy Warden in Bocas. He promised to do a total investigation. He knows Cher, and said he wants to find her.. He said he had nothing that I don't already know, but what he does know he gives to the Embassy and not to anyone else. I have spoken to a number of people who have already been interviewed. We are getting there.

I have a phone number for G bank, but need to find a Spanish Speaker. Maybe at the airport tomorrow.

Talk to you soon.

Mary

## June 17th Scott responded to Mary

From: Scott
To: Mary ; Alice ; John ; Judy; Henry
Sent: Thursday, June 17, 2010 7:25 PM
Subject: RE: Authorities re:Cher

Mary,
Sounds like good progress. You are really doing a great job. We all hope we solve this to a good end soon. Let me know if you need anything done.

Scott.

JUDY BARBER

### June 18th, 2010 A post on Cher's face book wall from Alice

Everything is helpful. Thanks so much for what ever you can send.
Alice June 18, 2010 at 6:24pm

### June 19th, 2010 a post on Cher's face book wall from Julie M.

Cher....whatcha doing? I want to come see you...call me or text asap....got LOTS to tell you...You will be happy for me....Love Ya Girl...Miss Ya
June 19, 2010 at 6:56pm

### June 21st Mary forward email to Alice
From: mary
Date: Mon, Jun 21, 2010 at 9:20 AM
Subject: Fwd: Global Bank Contact Info & List of Lawyers in Panama
To: Alice ; THOMAS

Hi

I can not crack the code to get to a person on this website. Maybe you computer geeks can get an email thru to the bank.

We need a person at the bank to tell us what info they need to tell us if Cher has an account with them. It will cost money to get an attorney or probably a subpeona. To avoid that, I am hoping Henry's name is on a record of some sort. HOW DO WE FIND THIS INFO???
Mary

This is the email mary forwarded

# A SISTER'S PROMISE

From: (Panama) <xxxx@state.gov>
Date: Thu, Jun 17, 2010 at 11:33 AM
Subject: Global Bank Contact Info & List of Lawyers in Panama
To: mary

Dear Mary

It was good to speak with you today. As promised, below please find contact details for G Bank and a list of lawyers here in Panama. Remember to email any questions about Cher's case to: panama-acs@state.gov Attention Consul General H C..

Take good care.
Regards,
Xxxxx
Consul
U.S. Embassy Panama

Global Bank Contact Details

## ⁓⁓⁓June 23rd, 2010 a post on Cher's face book wall from Sandy

Cher just in case. If you can see this message know that we the whole community are looking for you. Hang in we won't give up. Your jungle shopper amiga
June 23, 2010 at 7:45pm

## ⁓⁓⁓June 23rd I sent email to family

From: Judy
To: Alice ; Henry; Scott ; mary
Sent: Wednesday, June 23, 2010 9:06 PM
Subject: Re: Authorities re:Cher

## JUDY BARBER

doug has a friend that is from venezuala and speak spanish. do you have the contact info to the bank? we are going to get him to call and find out if cher had more than one bank account or find out as much as he can. doug just spoke to him and he is more than willing to help us.

### June 23rd sent email to Mary

On Wed, Jun 23, 2010 at 9:17 PM, Judy wrote:
Mary

do you have cher's social security number, date of birth and maybe my dad's as well. if Jose (the guy from venezuala) can ask those questions too.

what is the time zone difference? i am making a list of questions that Jose needs to ask in case i am not here. Jose meet cher when she was here so he knows about the island. cher had invited him and his brother to come to her island.

he said he will come tomorrow to just get the info together. i'm sure he will be able to find out a lot more by speaking the language.

### June 23rd received email from Mary

From: mary
To: Judy
Sent: Wednesday, June 23, 2010 9:55 PM
Subject: Fwd: G Bank Contact Info & List of Lawyers in Panama

As you can see, the US Embassy in Panama sent me an email with a website & phone number for G bank. I believe Cher put her big money there.

Then they sent a list of attorney's—another words, we need to get this information ourselves.

I so hope we can get clarification. WHAT DOES THE BANK NEED FROM US TO GET INFORMATION ON TRANSFER OF FUNDS FROM CHER'S ACCOUNTS?

From: mary
To: Judy
Sent: Wednesday, June 23, 2010 10:26 PM
Subject: Fwd: Cher Hughes

Judy,
This is the reply from me to US Embassy after they sort of blew me off that they were waiting on Panama Govt.
Between the mention of Bill Cortez and contacting congressman, I got a phone call the next day.
Attached is reply from Dave also.

Hope you can make sense of this.

Mary

---------- Forwarded message ----------
From: Dave
Date: Mon, Jun 7, 2010 at 3:22 PM
Subject: Re: Cher Hughes
To: mary

Mary,

I talked with lieza on friday, she is Chers best friend in cauchero. She said she was talking to Cher everyday, then spoke to her on a Monday, Cher said she was going to come to her house on Wednesday (in

## JUDY BARBER

Alimirante), from there they were supposed to travel to David to deal with car registration, etc. She never spoke to her again. She is very upset and feels that Cher would never not call or show up, she never heard anything about a guy or a sailing trip, she was only planning a trip to David on Wednesday.

One of the pieces of property that Cher supposedly sold is on Lieza's family's island. She said Cher told her she would never sell it or the island and that she would definitely know if she did.

She said if Cher would have gone sailing, she would know about it. She did not even receive a text.

I will contact the local police here to have them travel to Cauchero and ask the neighbors questions. The area is very remote and quiet. If something went on, someone will know something.

From what I have gathered talking to people around town is that Cher sent out a text stating..."met someone, going sailing, I'm OK."

She sent that to her old apartment manager (I forget her name, I will get it) and Sarah (who is not a drug addict and has known both myself and Cher for 20 years). She would have contacted Leiza to say she was leaving.

I received a text from Bill Cortez stating..."I have bought all property from Cher, including all things. No hard feelings, if you would like, I will bring you some of your stuff".

I find it very un-characteristic of Cher to sell the island, the house on Leiza's property, her boat, her car, and all her things and leave the dogs behind.

New Information I just recieved from a good friend of mine and Cher's, Sandi. About 3 months ago, Bill Cortez bought a house in Big Creek on Isla Colon from a guy named Bo Yancy, he has been a resident of Bocas for 8 years.

He has just been reported missing. His best friend, Doug, has not heard from him in months.
A text was sent from Bo to a few of his friends saying "I am out of here"

Bill Cortez and his wife have taken off. They left about 3 weeks ago and have not been seen since.

I believe her attorney is in David. I will get the authorities to contact her. If there was a transfer of property, she will know about it. Only the police can get information from the attorney.

I am going to have the police check with immigration. If Cher left the country, she will be registered.

I will continue to do research, question people, and work with the local police. I will give you a call in the next few days. The tone in Henry's voice the other day broke my heart.

Love, Dave

On Sat, Jun 5, 2010 at 2:55 PM, mary wrote:
Ms. M,

I spoke with you briefly on June 3. I am the Aunt of Cher Hughes, last seen in Bocas, Panama on March 17, 2010.. You wanted her address which I would like to provide. However, there IS no mailing address.

INFO I DO HAVE:

Cher Hughes
married to: Dave W
residing in: Bocas, Panama for 5 years, built & owned 2 duplex apartments, bought an island and built home on it.

## 🙦 JUDY BARBER

Birthdate: Nov., xx, xxxx
SS#: XXX-XX-XXXX
Florida DL# HXXXXXXXXXXXX 12/1/02
USPassport # XXXXXXXXX

Father is Henry Missouri Resident, phone XXX-XXX-XXXX, email: XXXXXX@aol.com
Husband is Dave H., email is:XXXXXX@gmail.com, phone is Panama #XXX-XXX-XXXX-XXXX.

She banks locally at Bank National in Bocas
She banks with big investments at Gl Bank, Panama City

Her last known sighting was with Shelly, Panamanian woman, mid 30's, . Cher had just made a cash transaction of about $600,000.00 with Bill Cortez, Panama cell phone #xxxxxx, email is xxxxxxPanama@yahoo.com. She sold property to him

Her lawyer's name is Julie xxxx. I am trying to get her phone number or at least which town she is in.

PLEASE UNDERSTAND: This information has been hard to come by, no one is forthcoming. I am in Texas, I do not speak Spanish. Her husband has been out of the picture, as they split up in October. They are not divorced. Her father is in St. Louis. We have been doing everything we can, but we need help from you.

I sent all this information to the US EMBASSY IN PANAMA CITY, xxxx. I emailed it to Sally at Panama-ACS@state.gov on April 29. I emailed photos on May 8. I emailed Sally with supplemental information on May 17.

On May 28, ACS in Panama emailed almost a form letter response saying they have not heard back from the Panamanian Government.

# A SISTER'S PROMISE

I do not intend to wait on the Panamanian Government to take action!!

Henry Has made contact with Congressman in Pevely Missouri, on June 4, 2010.
Dave has made a Police Report in Bocas with Officer Baker on May 21, 2010.

I spoke with you on June 3, and this email is dated June 5.

As you can imagine, we are very frustrated and desperate for help.

Our next plea will be the media.

Thank you in advance for any assistance you will provide.
Mary W------------Dave------
From: mary
To: Judy
Sent: Wednesday, June 23, 2010 11:01 PM
Subject: Re: JUDY

You should have all Cher;s info on the email to ACS Panama.

I think your Dad's social would be important, but Alice & Henry may not want to share it. You will have to ask them for it.
Mary

## June 28th received email from mary

From: mary
To: Judy ; Alice
Sent: Monday, June 28, 2010 2:36 PM
Subject: what's new

## JUDY BARBER

Hi
I am back home for 3days. We had someone make an offer on the house, but they want me to lose $17,000.

I plan to call the US Embassy in Panama tomorrow morning to see what i can learn.

I called Henry today. He is to call his banker & see if they can help him re:bank.
Any luck on your end?
Mary

## June 29th received email from Mary

From: mary
To: Alice ; Judy
Sent: Tuesday, June 29, 2010 10:01 AM
Subject: going to panama

Hi

I just got my schedule for July. I am off 12-20July.

Just called the Embassy, Dave & Henry. Am trying to set up meeting with Howard F. at the Embassy on July 13 (Tues) at the Embassy in Panama City. Dave said he will meet me there. Henry said he doesn't think he should go because his health is bad. I don't want him to go then, last thing I need is for health problems in a foreign country. I asked him to ask his bank for assistance on what I need on his behalf to get info from G Bank.

Cher has a little money with Henry if you need to go with me. I am ok going to Panama alone & meeting Dave .

However, I do not want to go to Bocas alone—I now know that I don't know who I am speaking with.

Hope to hear back today.

Mary

## June 30th, 2010 I sent email to Mary and Alice

From: Judy
To: Alice ; mary
Sent: Wednesday, June 30, 2010 8:06 PM
Subject: Re: going to panama

sorry i didn't get back with you. major health issues here. doug has been too sick to even leave the house for two days now. jennifer is going to be admitted to bayfront hospital tomorrow morning. her feet are the size of her thighs and they are turning black and blue. she was supposed to be admitted tonight but when she went there they didn't have the paperwork so she would have had to go thru emergency room again. BIG WASTE OF TIME AND MONEY. so she is going in the morning. she can hardly walk or speak. i pray they can help her & find out what the heck is going on. hopefully doug wont be having attacks tomorrow and can get to Jose (the spanish speaking guy) and have him call gl bank and get some information. i will keep you posted. love you guys. mary thanks again for all you are doing. i don't know what we would do without you.

### I received an email back from Mary

From: mary
To: Judy

## JUDY BARBER

Sent: Wednesday, June 30, 2010 10:02 PM
Subject: TAKE CARE OF YOURSELF TOO!!

Hi Judy!

Well at least we had Vegas!! Am so glad we had a few laughs (lots of laughs). We are both dealing with real life again, but take sometime everyday just to breathe.

Love ya' Mary

## July 3rd, 2010 I received an email from Mary

Date: Sat, Jul 3, 2010 at 2:40 AM
Subject: Newspaper article in Bocas re: Bo and Cher
To: mary

Missing Persons
Bocas residents Bo L. Barry Icelar, also known in Bocas as Bo Yancy and Cher Hughes have not been heard from in several months. If anyone has information as to their whereabouts, please contact the DIJ in Bocas (across from the airport entrance) or call (xx) 207-xxxx and speak to FBI Legal Attache P J.

## JUDY BARBER

### July 4th, 2010 a post on Cher's face book wall from Alice and Julie

Cher, I miss you. Please call me or dad. FYI—Jennifer is engaged!!!
July 4, 2010 at 8:29pm ·

Julie Cher...I MISS YOU AND LOVE YOU...
July 4, 2010 at 9:21pm

### July 7th, 2010 a post on Cher's face book wall from Da'Luna

CHER! where are you????
I miss you!
July 7, 2010 at 1:21am

### July 9th, 2010 Mary sent email to Family

Sent: Friday, July 9, 2010 12:34 PM
Subject: Trip to Panama
I just arrived to NYC, someone picked up my trip to Geneva. Am on return trip to STL. Alice and I will confer on Saturday, go to Panama City on Sunday.

Dave called and has reporters to meet us and accompany us to the Embassy. Sounded like a great idea.

S., Bo Yantee's sister (other missing American) just called. She does not want the press involved, is afraid that will run off the bad guys.

Will advise our decision after reflection. I will call FBI this afternoon for their input.

PLEASE PRAY—I am not this smart!!!

Mary

## July 11th, 2010 Mary sent email to Family

Sent: Sunday, July 11, 2010 9:59 PM
Subject: fyi

Just so you all know, we are safely in the Marriott on Sunday. As of now, plan to leave on Wed.

Have been in contact with Bo's best friend & attorney. He had no family. Has been missing person since Nov 29,'09. They are not happy with police non-action, however now that there are 2 missing persons they have more hope. That is a sad state! Mary

## July 12th, 2010 I sent an email to Mary

Sent: Monday, July 12, 2010 7:58 PM
Subject: Re: fyi

please be carefull this is such a scary thing and i pray that you & Alice can find the answers to cher and come home safe. i love you's. please keep us posted as i know that everyone is worried.

## July 13th, 2010 Mary sent email to family

Sent: Tuesday, July 13, 2010 12:05 AM
Subject: Panama City day 1

## JUDY BARBER

Alice & I are exhausted. Long day but very productive. We met Dave for breakfast, Don W., reporter for Panama Guide drove us to Prosecuting Attorney General's office to meet with The Man. Very formal, very productive. We convinced him to upgrade Cher's status from Missing Person (so many surfer's & crazy people are just missing here).to Criminal Investigation.

He sent us to Homicide Dectives to file official report under Dave's name, with total of 3 sworn interviews. We each had different, relevant information.

Don had photo of Bill Cortez, his vehicle with license plate #, his new name over Cher's rental property—it says "Casa Cortez, a delightfully wicked place" with a cross & skull as new logo.
The detectives hope to freeze all Cher's banking, cause a "criminal sequester of all Cher's property" because it was illegally obtained. And request Interpole to get a criminal background check on Bill Cortez.

Bad news is, we hear Bill is still near Bocas, will have access to who filed the complaint against him, and until his is apprehended—?

We were at police dept. with detectives, interpreters from 1pm til 8:30pm. We went to nice restaurant and celebrated a hard won victory.

Tomorrow we go to US Embassy. THEY HAVE DONE NOTHING!!! There was no missing person report on Bo Yantzee, we advised his status. All the information gathered in Bocas—people feel as if they were risking their lives to speak—this information had gone nowhere. but to an FBI file.

Many more fascinating details I hope to recall. For now, we are safe in our room. Tomorrow we go to advise the FBI & Embassy of the newly upgraded status—no thanks to them, but w will play nice for now.

Love, Thelma & Louise in the Marriott in Panama City!!

## ~~~July 13th, 2010 Mary sent email to Family

Sent: Tuesday, July 13, 2010 4:25 PM
Subject: day 2 Panama

Well, we accomplished a lot yesterday, which set things into motion today. Dave is getting phone calls from Bocas advising action. Dave provided LOTS of important info.

Today we went to the US Embassy & met with FBI. FBI Agent very astute, not forthcoming, but was already well informed and gleaned info from us that was relevant. Because of our actions yesterday, the case was bumped up to a higher level, (instead of another surfer running away from home). He now can work with his counterparts in the Panamania Govt, the Prosecuting Attorney General, etc.,
The US Embassy Consul is a total fool.

We are on the 10am flight from Panama to Houston tomorrow. I will be home for about 7 days. Mary

## ~~~July 14th, 2010 a post on Cher's face book wall from Julie

Hey Cher.....Girls need some FUN....Email me...I will send you my new number. I want to see you SOON...Love Ya Girl
July 14, 2010 at 11:16am

## ~~~July 15th, 2010 I sent an email to Mary and Alice

Sent: Thursday, July 15, 2010 7:52 PM
Subject: judy
just wanted to say THANK YOU BOTH for giving so much of yourself to help to find Cher.

## JUDY BARBER

i love you both and am glad to have you in my life.

love
Judy

## July 18ᵗʰ, 2010 a post on Cher's face book wall from Neydi

QUERIDA CHER, HOW ARE YOU?...WE MISS YOU!
LOVE,
NEYDI.
July 18, 2010 at 10:08pm

## July 18ᵗʰ 2010 11:53 a.m. Scott sent an email to everyone in contact list

Hello to all,
I am emailing you to ask you personally to take a moment, just a moment. Please.
to say a prayer, for the location of Cher Hughes (my niece, see attached photo). She has now been missing for months.
Please, I am asking you very seriously take just this moment.. one moment , right now..to say a prayer for her location that the authoritise find her and the persons responsible for her disapperance.
Cher and the family need your help in prayer now.. if you can take just a minute
The lord will come to our aid to locate Cher... Thank you so very much.
Thank you, Scott

Scott also posted the same message on face book

On July 20th the authorities had obtained enough evidence to be able to search the property that Wild Bill and his wife had stayed.

## JULY 20TH 2010 CHER'S BODY WAS FOUND

### July 20th, 2010 a post on Cher's face book wall from Dave

You r loved and will be missed by everyone that knew you.
July 20, 2010 at 10:45pm

## JULY 21ST 2010 I RECEIVED THE PHONE CALL I NEVER WANTED TO GET THEY FOUND CHER'S BODY

Cher had a Doberman pincher named Jack and much to everyone's amazement it was jack that actually found Cher. The property where Wild Bill lived, which is the same property Cher was buried, is about a mile and a half from the island where Cher lived. Her dog Jack would swim from Cher's island to that property every day. Wild Bill would take Jack back to Cher's place. When the authorities went to search for Cher, Jack was waiting there. Jack would approach the authorities bark several times and would run towards the top of a hill. Jack did not stop until someone followed him. Jack led the authorities right to where Cher was buried. When I was in Panama I actually went to that property and took that walk. It was not just right behind the house it was a hike thru the jungle on a slippery windy trail about three quarters of a mile. At the top of the hill was a clearing and it looked like it was used to dump trash. It was only a miracle and the grace of god that Cher was found. Jack laid down right on top of the grave that Cher was in. He knew she was there. I have never witnessed such a strong bond and love between a human and an animal. It is just another sign to me as to what a unique individual my sister was. She loved her animals and they knew it. Jack became a hero in Bocas Del Toro. He was in many newspaper articles and was even in a parade Jack still lives in Bocas Del Toro. He is still being cared for by Cher's friend. I would love to have him to take care of, but I could not change the life that he knows. He is used to the island life and being able to run free.

*Jack swam from Cher's house to the Holbert (Brown) house*

A SISTER'S PROMISE

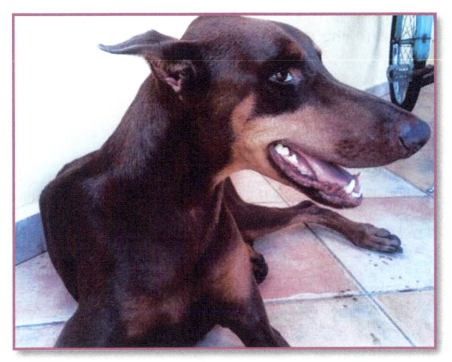

*JACK A TRUE HERO*

This is a picture of the most incredible dog I have ever meet. He is a true hero. Thank you Jack for loving my sister.


The following were post on Cher's face book from friends

Cher bear We pray that you are at peace
That you find yourself in Gods hands
July 21, 2010 at 8:30am

REST IN PEACE AMIGA.
July 21, 2010 at 1:13pm

Justin

## ❦ JUDY BARBER

Rest in peace Cher!
July 21, 2010 at 12:10pm

Lindsey
I will remember you always , my dear sweet beautiful friend, love you cher bear xoxooxxoxoxoxxoxoxo!!!!!!!!!!!
July 21, 2010 at 10:25am
Ozden i am very sorry :( we did not sleep last night !!!
July 21, 2010 at 10:26am
Lindsey can't stop crying this morning, bless and love to her family, not fair..... discusting, angry!!
July 21, 2010 at 10:29am

I love you Cher. Thank you for all the memories, you are a great friend and I will miss you always.
My ship sails from darkness to light,
July 21, 2010 at 5:48pm

Dyllan
Rest in peace sweet Cher, you will always be remembered with much love
July 21, 2010 at 2:16pm
Mackenze
RIP Cher...

They'll find that monster and avenge you.
July 21, 2010 at 1:29pm

CHERRRRRRRRRRR!!! :/
I Will miss you So much Hunny!!
Thanks for all the memories and the great times we had together!!
I love youuu!! and i will allways miss you, and your beautiful smile!
♥ ♥ ♥
R.I.P!
July 21, 2010 at 9:12pm

Brenda
Thank you for the biggest adventure of my life. I will always remember you and your love of the world. The smile on your face donating to the children, a memory I will have forever. God Bless Mary for fighting for you.
July 21, 2010 at 8:26pm

Cookie
words are not enough to express this
July 21, 2010 at 6:49pm

## July 21st, 2010 I sent an email to Dave

Sent: Wednesday, July 21, 2010 6:00 PM
Subject: judy

hi Dave. I'M SO SORRY i can't believe this is happening. i wish we could be there together. i know you feel lost as i do. i have so many thoughts going thru my mind. i do want to do what cher would have wanted and have some of her ashes on the island then bring her home to me. i will take her home. she saved me and brought me to florida and i will take her home.

i can't type any more right now. i just can't take it.

love you
Judy


I fell apart and cannot even remember how I made it through the next few days.
I could not sleep. I could not eat. There was nothing I could do but cry and scream.

## JUDY BARBER

How could this have happened? Thank god for working for my old boss Matt because he understood. I actually had tried to go to work and Matt once again sent me home. He had called me in his office and this is what I remember he said "Judy I remember how upset you were when Cher moved away to Panama. I think you should go home and take whatever time you need. Do not worry about your job we will handle your work for you. I am truly sorry for what has happened to your sister."

It meant a lot to me to not have to worry about work. I was so confused and lost and the support was very comforting. THANK YOU MATT

## July 22, 2010 a post on Cher's face book wall from Alice

Thank you all for posting your sentiments, prayers and beautiful remembrances of Cher. Each of us has a part of her, our own little stories. She touched so many people and loved you all—we will always be a part of her.
July 22, 2010 at 9:32pm
I have many memories of Cher, but what I remember the most is how she had a special kindness and love for children. My daughter was the first of many nieces and nephews and the memory I have most is Cher couldn't wait to see her. There was a time we were almost kicked out of a store because we were making too much noise. We were playing with all the toys and I do mean ALL. If you can imagine… all the windup toys were running around, whatever played music was turned on, the bouncing balls were everywhere and the riding toys? Well… we would put my daughter on them and race down the aisle. We would laugh so hard we would cry.
July 22, 2010 at 9:34pm

Linda
Our hearts are out to your family
July 22, 2010 at 3:40pm

## July 22nd, 2010 a post on Cher's face book wall from Alice

http://www.fox2now.com/videobeta/1d849e53-2743-485f-9650-f46ea0bb8092/News/Sunset-Hills-Woman-Murdered-in-Panama
July 22, 2010 at 11:04pm


## July 23rd, 2010 a post on Cher's face book wall from Graceila

OH CHER!!!...ITS HARD TO BELIEVE IT!!!...I´LL MISS YOU MY LOVELY FRIEND!!!...REST IN PEACE!!...
July 23, 2010 at 4:12pm


## July 26th 2010 received an email from Uncle Jim

Sent: Monday, July 26, 2010 5:52 PM
Subject: THEY CAUGHT THE BASTARDS WHO MURDERED CHER HUGHES

YOU CAN READ ARTICLE AT
WWW.PANAMA-GUIDE.COM


## July 26th, 2010 more post on Cher's face book wall from Cher's friends

i am glad to hear that the scum who did this and his wife have been arrested
July 26, 2010 at 4:09pm

cher you got him, I know you are near
July 26, 2010 at 5:56pm

## ॐ JUDY BARBER

As I read all these post I was proud of the fact that I had a sister
That had truly touched so many lives. The post continued on.

Julie posted a picture of Cher's with her grandson. She was a very close
Friend on Cher's that lived in Florida. Cher would see Julie when she came to
Visit.

She always did like them young!!! Cher and my grandson sleeping... can you believe she woke up and actually got dressed and went out???
July 26, 2010 at 7:37pm
Laura likes this.
Michele I hope the jails in CR and Panama suck ass so those animals suffer.
July 26, 2010 at 7:43pm
Julie they should go straight to HELL.
July 26, 2010 at 7:54pm
Michele In the most painful way!
July 26, 2010 at 7:56pm
Lynn This is so awful...I hope they rott in HELL in jail down there.

The prisons are worse so I've heard. Going to actual HEll would be to good for these bastards.
July 27, 2010 at 12:06am
Julie Yes we will miss her Art...I found some photo's of her I took at your house that night you cooked us that FABULOUS dinner!!!
July 27, 2010 at 12:02pm

## July 28th 2010 I emailed Scott

Sent: Wednesday, July 28, 2010 9:43 PM
Subject: judy

Hi Scott,
sorry it took so long to get back in touch with you, i've been trying to deal with this whole thing. i can't believe it but i am thanking god that they have been caught. i believe that cher has once again helped a lot of people in her death.

i wrote a poem that i would love for you to read at her service. i want to thank you for all you have done and know that i will be there in my heart. i am having a service for cher here as well.

i have spoken to Dave and he has promised me he will bring some of her ashes to florida so all the friends she has here will have a chance to say our goodbyes.

i thank god that i was able to share her last birthday with her when she was here. i have found memories and a beautiful bedroom to sleep in that she helped me with. she made it a point not to leave florida until she had a room built for me. it's been very hard to handle but i know that she would want me to be strong and that is what i am going to do. i will always have her in my heart and know she is with me every night when i go to sleep.

### JUDY BARBER

please let me know when you decide to have her service. i will keep in touch and let you know as well when i plan to have it here.

thanks again Scott. words just can't explain how much this means to me. i love you
love always judy

### I received an email back from Scott

Sent: Wednesday, July 28, 2010 10:39 PM
Subject: RE: judy

Thanks for your words and thoughts
I will share you poem with all at the service
will let you know as soon as arranged.
love you
Scott

### July 29th, 2010 10:28pm I posted a face book message to everyone

i'm having a get together on saturday morning to go thru pictures and plan the service for cher. i want to have cher's service at gulfport beach at the pravillion. i know she had a lot of good friends and if you would like to come over to my house and share your ideas you are welcome. my address is …. i was thinking around 10 am

### July 31st, 2010 I had a few of Cher's friends come over to go through

Pictures and make photo arrangements for the service. I thought this would be a great way to show how much Cher loved and enjoyed spending time with friends.

A SISTER'S PROMISE

We took the following picture when we were done. It was amazing to me the ray of sunshine that came through the window was directly on the shells we put together to form the letter C. This picture has NOT been altered.

## ~~~~~July 31st, 2010 11:25am I sent Dave a message on face book

Judy wrote on Dave timeline.
"hey Dave i'm so glad the bastard is confessing so that the other families can have some type of closure as well. we are at the house right now looking at pictures and trying to plan some type of service for her. of course we are going to wait for you but i want to have it all planned. i love you and hope you are ok."

## JUDY BARBER

### July 31st, 2010 I received face book message from Mary

July 31, 2010 at 1:16pm

Hi Judy, Hope you are having a peaceful day with photos. Our girl sure crammed a lot of fun into her life! She is my hero. I hope to make it to the service at Gulfport if I can. Big hi to Jen, hope she is feeling better. Take care of you! Take a lesson from Cher! Smile!

### July 31st, 2010 received an email from Scott

Date: Saturday, July 31, 2010, 4:41 PM

We will be having a small gathering of family and friends at our home here in St.Louis to celebrate and remember Cher.....
Sunday
August, 8th
1 to 4 pm
With a prayer service at 1:30
If you can not attend, I know you will all be there in spirit and prayer.
With love to all, Scott and Ronda

### August 1st, 2010 I emailed Scott

From: Judy
To: Scott
Sent: Sunday, August 1, 2010 9:55 AM
Subject: Re: St. Louis Gathering for Cher

thank you so much for taking care of this for cher. i know she is with us in spirit. i am having a service for her saturday august 7th by the ocean which is where i know she loved to be. Dave is trying to get cher's body on monday, have her cremated on tuesday then fly here to florida on friday. so please say a prayer that they will release her now. they keep telling him tomorrow, tomorrow but i know if we all pray then god will answer. i love you and wish i could be there with the family. love judy

### August 1st, 2010 received an email from Scott

Date: Sunday, August 1, 2010, 12:13 PM

Thanks for the update, we will be one in spirit on Saturday and Sunday.
Remember the gatherings are for Chers "life" not death.
she is in the most wonderful place.... in the arms of our lord.. like a babe, he holds her close to his heart...
believe this ... believe in her total happiness in his arms...
With love,
Scott and Ronda

### August 2nd, 2010 11:44 am I received face book from Nicole

hey judy is the service for cher going to be this coming saturday? i heard tht Dave is bringing her to florida need to know so i can get off work.... thnks and my prayers are with u all look foward to seeing u...

### August 4th, 2010 I received a face book message from Mary

Hi Judy, I am trying to get thru red tape and get Cher's body released to Dave without all this foolishness. Hope to have answers soon. Sam, Becky, Carol & I are driving to STL on Fri for service on Sun. Will advise when I know more. How are you doing?
August 4, 2010 at 10:33am

## JUDY BARBER

Aug 4, 2010 at 2:59 PM,
Thomas commented on your wall post:

"Hi Mary... I don't understand why the FBI is now involved and requires DNA evidence to release Cher's body to the family. The last thing we were told by Dave is the Panama Authorities were waiting for Cher's dental records to confirm Cher's identity. Further, I am curious why they have not contacted Cher's father Henry or Cher's sister Alice who has legal Power Of Attorney for their father, Henry . Maybe Alice is the right person to cut through all your red tape. The FBI and U.S. Embassy in Panama have a copy of the POA on file. Why don't you give Alice a call and let her get things done. "

### Scott posted a face book reply

Scott wrote:
Let Dave, (and Mary if her help is needed) work on it with the authorities. I trust they are doing all they can to move thing as smoothly as possible with all those involved.
August 4, 2010 at 4:16pm

Mary
Thomas, flights leave for Panama 3 times a day.
August 4, 2010 at 4:18pm

### Thomas posted a face book reply

Thomas Hey... keep up the great work...! I was only suggesting that since Alice has POA for Henry... maybe we could expedite matters, save someone a trip to Panama, and get closure for the family. For the record Mary... there are several flights to Panama every day on more than one airline.
August 4, 2010 at 5:06pm

## ⁓August 5th, 2010 I received a face book message from Nicole

okay so definitely no service this saturday!!! ???? okay thanks a lot.....
August 5, 2010 at 1:23pm

### My response

i can't have a service for cher until she is here. i will keep you posted. i know she would want you there. I'm doing my best to do what is right. love judy
August 5, 2010 at 7:49pm

### Nicole responded

Nicole i understand thanks for keeping us updated... my dad said he may be given u a call about it...love ya
August 6, 2010 at 6:16pm

## ⁓August 6th, 2010 I sent a face book message to Cher's friend Paula

hi Paula,
i am cher's sister judy here in st petersburg, i am planning on having a service for cher on the 21st on gulfport beach. i just have to do something for her by the water. i really think she would love that. family & friends from out of town can get a flight round trip with advance notice flying out on the 19th & returning on the 22nd. i really appreciate your offer of letting them stay at your motel. i am sooooooo devastated and can't believe that this has happened to her. can you please give me your number or call me at home or cell. i really need to get things arranged and need all the help i can get. i am not sure

how many rooms you have available and it will probably be about 5. cher had a lot of people in her life that love her. cher has sent me many blessings and i truly believe you are one as well. hope to speak to you soon. thanks judy

## August 6th, 2010 8:18pm I sent Dave a face book message

Judy wrote on Dave's timeline.
"am so heart broken and i miss her soo much. i want to have a service for her on the 21st on the water. i am thinking gulfport beach around 5pm. i want to see the sunset on the water. i will never forget the first time i saw the ocean and it was with cher. she moved me here to florida and without her i would of never... had the experiences, laughter & joy in my life that i have had. i am thankful that i got to share the time that i had with her. i'm proud to say CHER'S MY SISTER. i pray for all of us to be able to handle this. I'M JUST LOST."

## A SISTER'S PROMISE

### August 6th, 2010 8:27pm I posted a face book message to everyone

All I could do at this point was just copy and paste what I sent to Dave. I needed to let everyone know the day I wanted to have the service.

SO heart broken. i miss her SOO much i want to have service on the 21st on water. i am thinking gulfport beach about 5pm. i want to see sunset on the water. i will never forget first time i saw the ocean and it was with CHER. she moved me to florida and without her i would never had experiences, laughter & joy in life that i had. i'm thankful to share the time that i had with her. i'm proud to say CHER'S MY SISTER.

### August 7th, 2010 I sent a face book message to Keli

From: Judy
Sent: Saturday, August 7, 2010 10:06 AM
Subject: Re: Keli commented on your status...

HI Keli,
i wanted it to be the 14th but we don't think cher will be here by then. it's to much for my aunt to fly to panama on monday then give dna then if they release cher she will be cremated then try and catch a flight out. it just too much. so sam called & said they found a flight round trip from springfield mo to florida for $80 bucks. i want to make sure everyone can come and for all the people up north to try and get a flight with a two day notice just wont work. i pray she will be here by the 21st but if not we will still have a service and then i will have another one and of course you can be there. i just have to get something planned i can't take not doing anything. love ya

## JUDY BARBER

### Keli replied back to me

To: "Judy
Date: Saturday, August 7, 2010, 3:47 AM

"judy hey she loved u to ,you are and will always be her baby sis ... i cant believe she is gone i miss her to ...cant stop crying .. judy u let me know if there is anything i mean anything i will be there for u just want u to know that k..and please let me know when service will be i thought is was the 14th now its the 21st?? i love u judy .

### August 7$^{th}$, 2010 I received a face book message from Travis, Cher's neighbor and friend for many years.

To: "Judy
Date: Saturday, August 7, 2010, 10:11 PM

Travis commented on your status:

"judy i agree i remember the day she moved here i miss her soo much she is everywhere i look i feel her with me but im soo sad"

### August 8$^{th}$, 2010 I received another face book message from Travis

Sent: Sunday, August 8, 2010 9:41 AM
Subject: Re: Travis commented on your status...

i know that everyone is hurting. they are having a service for cher today in st louis. i can't stop crying & thinking of how blessed i've been to have her. I MISS HER SOO MUCH

## August 8th, 2010 10:04 am I posted a face book message to everyone

Today is the service in St. Louis for my beautiful loving sister cher. i'm so devastated and just can't stop crying. i looked so forward to going and finally seeing her in panama. she spent october & november with me and after all these years i finally got my passport and plane ticket to go on May 1st with my aunt mary. I never got to go she was already gone.
i feel so hurt that i didn't go sooner. why did i wait so long. now i will never have the chance to enjoy the paradise with her that she told me so much about. i can't explain the hurt that i am feeling. I MISS HER. i want to hear her call me BABY SISTER and have fun with her. she always made me have fun it was her nature to make sure we all laughed. life will never be the same.

## August 8th, 2010 3:42pm I posted on my wall on face book

Judy added a new photo to the album cher.

cher
"Home arrangement 8-8-10. Even the sun lights up the seashells."

## August 9th, 2010 a post on Cher's face book wall from Tammy

### ❦ JUDY BARBER

Hi Cher,
I still can not believe it all. I went to your Mermorial today here in St. Louis, it was very nice and you are so very loved. It was nice exchanging photos and stories and although I did not get to physically go to your island, I did see many photos and can see why you loved it so much. You truely made the best and most of your life and touched so very many people. I will miss your very, very much my dear friend. I will never forget you, you rocked my world and I will love you forever. As your sister said in her Poem to you, Heaven must have needed a blue eyed angel and I will take comfort in knowing that you will be amongst my angels, helping to watch over me and so many of your loved ones. Please kiss my loved ones for me and share that beautiful smile. You are in my heart and etched in my mind, till we meet again, I love you! Tammy :)
August 9, 2010 at 12:11am

## ~~~August 9th, 2010 received an email from Tammy

Hi Judy,'I was just going over some of Cher messages between us and ran across this one, just thought I would send it to you. It was after her and Dave broke up.

Cher Hughes December 2, 2009 at 6:23pm
i love you too....i just came back from florida as my sister judy has same problem....so we went out and had fun....she is so much fun i love her...she makes me laugh...she is on face book...judy August 9, 2010 at 1:00am

## ~~~August 9th, 2010 received a face book message from Nicole

hey judy!!! you need to get in contact with my aunt sher my dads sis, she can give you much help with food for the service from foxys!!!! i

## A SISTER'S PROMISE

have already told her about the situation and she is glad to help she has all the special containers and things to keep food warm,, she caters a lot for weddings and all kinds of things....and can easily help you out with everything she just needs to know what your wanting and what not, i will message you her phone number, please don't hesitate to call she is waiting for you, she will def help you make a special service for cher bear.. hope this helps love you nicole :)
August 9, 2010 at 1:23pm

### August 9th, 2010 7:39 pm Paula posted a comment on face book

I heard there will be a memorial service for Cher in St. Pete, FL. I will be there, so please let me know when the arrangements are made.

Also, I would like to offer complimentary accommodations at my hotel for you, your family, and Cher's family, if our location is suitable. P...lease let me know the date(s) as soon as you know so I can block the rooms(s).

You are in my thoughts and prayers.
Love,
Paula

### August 9th, 2010 8:02pm I posted a face book message to everyone

to all planning to travel to florida and need accomodations for cher's service on the 21st please let me know. i have left a message for Paula and will be talking to her tomorrow. i did confirm that there a plenty of rooms available. so i can reserve them tomorrow. just need to get a number of rooms. thanks judy

## JUDY BARBER

### ~~~~August 10ᵗʰ, 2010 7:11 am I posted a message on face book to everyone

i am calling Paula and reserving rooms. Sam has offered to do the service. i'm still wanting to do something on the beach. i don't think with the weather and the heat trying to have food is a good idea. so if i have it around 6:00 on saturday everyone can eat before that. i will update everyone when i get home from work. love to all and thanks for being there.

### ~~~~August 10ᵗʰ, 2010 Mary sent an email to the family

Sent: Tuesday, August 10, 2010 2:30 PM
Subject: Panama trip

Hi,
Am waiting to board flight PTY/IAH/EWR. Been runnig since I landed yesterday. Am working flight to Copenhagen tomorrow.

YES, they needed my DNA, still need a certified birth certificate. However, there will be a long delay before releasing the remains.

A lot more information was learned, will advise later.

Dateline show was here, Dave & I did an interview this morning. They are going to Bocas & Island tomorrow. I thought it went well.

Love, Mary

### ~~~~August 10ᵗʰ, 2010 Scott forward an email from Sam

# A SISTER'S PROMISE

From: Scott
sent: Tuesday, August 10, 2010 6:09 PM
Subject: FW: shared a link on your Wall...

Date: Tue, 10 Aug 2010 14:12:16 – 0700
To: Scott
From: xxx@facebookmail.com
Subject: shared a link on your Wall...

shared a link on your Wall.

http://www.facebook.com/l/f30dc;www.youtube.com/watch?v=CViw0uKoyjE
In February of 2008, Scott (my uncle) and I went to Bocas del Toro to visit my cousin Cher and her husband Dave. These are some of the photos I took on that trip. Cher had a huge heart and a bright smile. All of her family and friends will miss her greatly, and remember her always! We love you Cher! The song "Angel from Montgomery" by John Prine can be purchased here: http://itunes.apple.com/us/album/angel-from-montgomery/id3858390?i=3858336

This is a beautiful tribute to Cher that Sam our cousin put together. As I watched it I could not help but think of how much it meant to Cher to be able to share her
Paradise with her loved ones. The smile of her face tells it all.

## August 10th, 2010 I received a face book message from Sam

Hey guys, looking forward to seeing you all. Judy, thanks for setting the date, we now have secured our airline tickets and are set to go. Mom, Dad, my wife and kids, brother, wife and kids are all coming. I am writing the sermon for the service and Shawn is working on something special we can do on the beach, like a candlelight or flower

release in the ocean. I think Cher would like that. Dave, Travis and Keli, help Judy get the word out to everyone down there, I know she is overwhelmed right now. Judy, I believe you said around 6pm on the 21st, but maybe Shawn can start a face book memorial profile that we can all send out to everyone. Love you guys and looking forward to seeing you all.
August 10, 2010 at 6:50pm

## August 11th, 2010 I received a face book message from Paula

Judy,
God has sent you to me and me to you. We will honor Cher, your dear sister and my dear friend appropriately.

### I responded to Paula on face book

From: Judy
sent: Thursday, August 12, 2010 7:07 AM
Subject: Re: Paula you a message on Face book...

thank you so much. i know god will guide us and help us thru. my life is forever changed. i miss her so much. thank you again for all you are doing. you are truely an angel.
"thank you Paula. The service for cher will be SATURDAY the 21st. i just want to make sure you can be there and anyone else that has been blessed enough to have known my sister."

## August 12th, 2010 7:13 am I posted a face book message to everyone

making the arrangements for cher's service. it will be SATURDAY the

21st. i will let everyone know the details but anyone that has been blessed enough to know my sister is welcome to come. i know she has touched many lives and she still is. i will give everyone the details when i have confirmed everything. THANK YOU TO ALL THAT ARE HELPING and for all of you that are praying for us.

### August 12, 2010 sent face book message to Mary

hey mary,
just wanted to say thank you for all you have done. cher's service is on the 21st saturday. if you think you can make it i would love for you to be here. everyone is welcome. you know our cher she always loved a crowd. i am so thankful to have you in my life. you have really done an amazing job. thanks for being the person that you are. i love you

### August 12th, 2010 7:28pm I commented on face book to Sam http://www.youtube.com/watch?v=CViw0uKoyjE&feature=player_embedded

Judy commented on a link.

Cher Hughes Remembered
gdata.youtube.com
"that was so amazing. what an awesome job. cher would be proud. thank you so much. it is comforting to know how much cher is loved."

### August 12, 2010 7:48pm I posted on face book to everyone

i know have conformation on cher's service. it will be at the don cesar on st. pete beach. we have the SUNSET PAVILLON. we have the area from 5-9. the service for cher will start at 6:00 i would love everyone to watch the sunset together in memory of Cher. please tell every-

one you know that knew cher to come to the service. EVERYONE IS WELCOME. cher always loved a big crowd. i don't have everyone's contact information so please help me get the word out.
7:51pm
Judy updated her status.
"the picture i attached is one that cher took on her camera. she was at the don cesar before she went back to panama. i am thankful to have the service for her there. hope everyone will come."
8:11pm
Judy updated her status.
"i also wanted to let everyone know that this will be casual. be prepared to walk in the sand to the water for sunset."

## August 13th, 2010 8:22pm I posted on face book

"not enough words to say how much i miss cher."

8:23pm
Judy added a new photo to the album Wall Photos.

8:25pm
Judy updated her status.
"cher before she left in my room"

## August 14, 2010 received message from Mary

Hi Judy, I would love to come. No promises as I am scheduled to work. I know it will be lovely memorial. I am so pleased the C.'s will be there too. We can put an end to this soon, to look forward to happier days. TAKE CARE OF YOURSELF. Love, Mary

## August 14th, 2010

Somebody posted on face book an interview that was done previously at the prison in Panama called LA JOYA. This is the prison that Wild Bill will be sent to when he is convicted. This is no jail like this here in America. This is the place he needs to spend the rest of his life. I still say even when he is convicted it will not stop the
Pain in my heart. I will live with this forever.

## August 14th, 2010 I commented on a post on face book
11:16am
Judy commented on a link.

La Joya—The Jewel
gdata.youtube.com
http://www.youtube.com/watch?v=OD_Vhvh_HV4
"i hope both of them feel the pain that they have caused to so many people. i hope they are tortured everyday. i will have to live my life without my siser that i loved so much. there still isn't enough punishment for that kind of pain but at least they are not in the states at the resorts we have here."

I spoke with Shawn over the phone and we discussed how nice it would be to have Don attend the service for Cher in St. Petersburg Florida. Don had
Played a very big part of helping to get things moving to find Cher. I will always be grateful to him. He truly was a god send in our time of need. Thank you DON.

## AUGUST 14TH, 2010 Shawn sent out a Face book message to everyone

## JUDY BARBER

We are trying to cover Don's expenses for a flight to St Petersburg, FL to attend Cher's memorial service. This is a man who is primarily responsible for the capture of a serial killer that murdered our friend Cher and many more. As of yesterday, Don was able to positively link the killer to a body found in Costa ...Rica in 2007. If you have been touched by this mans hard work and dedication, please take a moment to contribute. Just enter don@panama-guide.com in the "TO" field, select "US Dollars" and select "Gift"

Don travel expense fund... Lets get Don to Cher's Memorial Service personal.paypal.com
Follow the link... get your debit/credit card ready. Just enter don@panama-guide.com in the

"TO" field, select "US Dollars" and select "Gift". Any amount will help! Don is going to update me on the contributions. Thank You, Shawn
August 14, 2010 at 3:54pm

## August 15, 2010 sent face book message to Alice and Thomas

hey Thomas & Alice, have you heard anything about if cher's body has been released? i wrote Dave a couple times but haven't heard. i'm still planning cher's service but i would like to know if she is going to be here. this is so tuff. thank you guys for all you have done. i just want to let you know i'm proud to say you're my family. love ya

## August 15th, 2010 I posted a face book message to everyone

it would really be nice to be able to thank don in person, this could be our only chance. i will make sure he has a room at the motel. please help if you can. without don we may never of had the chance

to know what happened to our cher. he is a hero and has been a blessing to all of us. thanks
August 15, 2010 at 10:02am

## ⁓August 16th, 2010 Sam posted a message on Face book

Sam Just donated 20. If we can get 30 people to donate 20, that will get him here and back.
August 16, 2010 at 2:15pm

## ⁓August 16th, 2010 Shawn posted a message of Face book

Please help Don W. get to Cher's Memorial.... any amount will help. Thank You, Shawn

Shawn Judy, I know you and Thomas put in already... just trying to get the message to everyone on your friends list.
August 15, 2010 at 1:08pm

Sam Just donated 20. If we can get 30 people to donate 20, that will get him here and back. Didnt you say it was five hundred something?
August 16, 2010 at 2:15pm

August 16, 2010 received a face book message back from Thomas

Hi Judy... Sorry for the slow reply... Don't spend too much time looking at FB. Alice told me that you and her spoke on the phone. I did see the photos of the memorial that you put together for Cher... Very Beautiful. The services at the hotel and beach will be perfect. You are doing such a wonderful job. Cher is smiling upon us all from heaven... especially upon her Baby Sister.

## JUDY BARBER

### August 16th 2010 received email from Dave

----- Forwarded Message -----
From: Dave
To: Judy
Sent: Monday, August 16, 2010 6:48 PM
Subject: Fwd: Dateline NBC

---------- Forwarded message ----------
From: A., Beth (NBC Universal) <Xxx. A.@nxxxx.com>
Date: Mon, Aug 16, 2010 at 1:37 PM
Subject: RE: Dateline NBC
To: Dave

Hi Dave,

Thanks for chatting with me earlier. I wanted to follow up our conversation with an email to ask if it would be okay with Cher's sister and family if we filmed Cher's memorial service in St. Petersburg this coming Saturday. We're hoping to use some of the memorial in our piece as a further illustration of how much Cher was loved.

We will be extremely unobtrusive—only ask that we are able to link our microphone to the podium microphone (if there is one) so we can capture the audio of any eulogies given.

I'm happy to speak to any of Cher's family and assuage any concerns. My cell is xxxxxxx.

Thanks so very much.
Beth

Beth

xx Rockefeller Plaza
NY, NY xxxxx

—

Dave

## August 16th, 2010

I was interviewed by reporters for Channel 8 news. They aired a piece on Cher at 11:00 pm news.

## August 16, 2010 I sent a face book email to everyone

we were just interviewed by channel 8. they are going to show it on the 11:00 news tonight. they are also putting cher's story into the tampa tribune tomorrow. i was glad to get to tell everyone how wonderful my sister is. even the reporter said it just sad how this person could have caused so much hurt to so many people and not even have a regret. he even said he hopes he rotes in prison.
August 16, 2010 at 7:33pm

here is the link for the channel 8 news

http://www.facebook.com/l/8a1d9;TBO.com: Serial killer caught
http://www.facebook.com/l/8a1d99yPDmLE19Ds7G4006AA49Q;www2.tbo.com/video/2010/aug/16/serial-killer-caught-11855/video-news/

A Bay area family is grieving the loss of a woman who may be the victim of a suspected serial killer caught in Panama.

## August 17th, 2010 I sent an email to my friend at work

## ❦ JUDY BARBER

From: Judy
To: Marie
Sent: Tuesday, August 17, 2010 7:16 AM
Subject: judy

hey Marie,

can you please let everyone know that the service for cher will be at the don cesar on saturday. we have the sunset pravillon from 5 to 9. the service will start at 6:00 pm

we are going to watch the sunset and release some balloons in memory of my sister.
everyone is welcome.
thanks for all your thoughts & prayers. this is really a tough thing to go thru, but i know my sister is looking over me and giving me the strength i need to carry on.

love ya's
Judy

## August 17th, 2010 I received an email from Mary

From: mary
To: Judy
Sent: Tuesday, August 17, 2010 9:13 AM
Subject: Newspaper article

Hi Judy,
I just read the article. You did a great interview. The facts were correct, and Cher was in a positive light. I am always worried they will get morbid, but this was great—hope you are satisfied. I wish they hadn't put his photo on there, but it is the story.

I finally figured how to put $$ for Don's travel on the account. Later today, when I get my personal computer up, I am going to add $200.00 to your checking account. I know you will put it towards what you need. Please take care of yourself—don't do everything on your own.

On another note, Alice and I have totally different feelings toward Dave. She is certainly entitled to her feelings. However, he did not kill Cher. Bill Cortez did. We all know he left her and was with another woman, no one needs to tell you & me that men can be dicks! I do know, when we realized Cher was really missing, Dave stepped up and signed the accusation of murder. This truly could have been a death sentence for him. This case could never have been solved without Dave's participation. Alice and Henry seem to think because they don't like Dave they can discredit him, even implicate him in the murder and get access to the land and money. I have been totally SHOCKED by some of their actions. I called Henry to apologize if he thought I over stepped my bounds (but really, what was he doing but kicking furniture & stomping around?) I hate to have to tell you that conversation did not end well. He said Cher would not have been murdered if Dave had been home where he belonged. He forgot who he was talking to. I replied that he was the last person to pass judgement—a lot went down on his watch because he wasn't where he should have been years ago. Thank God for Sam C Some of the men in our lives have failed us, but we are strong women and I don't want to be divided. I am not asking you to take sides. I have heard the term "Cher's team", am not sure exactly what that means as I hoped everyone is on Cher's team even if they don't like each other. We can talk this out later, or never. I just thought I needed to share some of the "behind the scenes". I believe a united front for the public and friends is another way to honor Cher, I wouldn't want my marriage to be open for scrutiny.

I hope a will is found and there can be clarity on what Cher wanted. During my investigations, I could not get access to bank or person-

## JUDY BARBER

al information (I was trying to see if anything was accessed and by whom). I could not even find her lawyers. The story should bring them to the surface.

Again, my reason for sharing is to keep you informed. I don't need a reply, but if you want me to call, let me know. You don't need to be involved in any drama and I am sorry if this caused you any pain. Please know my intentions have always been good. Even if my mouth gets me in trouble. Love you.

Mary

## August 17th, 2010 I sent out a face book email

just interviewed by abc action news. they will show the interview at 11:00 tonight.
August 17, 2010 at 9:12pm

## August 18th 2010, I received an email from Mary

From: mary
To: Judy
Sent: Wednesday, August 18, 2010 1:26 PM
Subject: Fwd: Photos of Cher

Dear Xxx,
Hello. I m in Dublin working right now. I am taking the liberty of forwarding this message to Cher's youngest sister, Judy B. She is organizing the Memorial Service in Florida. Whatever she says, I concur. Thank you for presenting our girl in the best light.
Mary

---------- Forwarded message ----------
From: A., Xxx (NBC Universal) <Xxx. A.@xxxxxi.com>
Date: Wed, Aug 18, 2010 at 3:17 PM
Subject: Photos of Cher
To: mary.

Hi Mary,

Tina passed along your information. I'm the NY producer working along with Charmian for the Dateline hour on Cher. Just finished watching your interview—you spoke so beautifully about Cher.

I'm writing to ask if it would be okay with the family if Dateline came to the memorial service being held in St Petersburg this weekend. We'd ideally like to capture a bit of the memorial on film along with some eulogies or memories that friends and family might share. I'm happy to speak with you further if you have any questions or concerns—please let me know a good time to call.

I'm also emailing to ask for some pictures and/or video of Cher through the years. If there is another family member I should reach out to please do let me know—we, of course, would like to represent her as she was through the photos and videos her loved ones cherish most

Thanks so very much.

My kindest regards,
Beth

Beth
Dateline NBC
xxx. A.@nbcuni.com

## JUDY BARBER

### August 18, 2010 I sent out face book email

http://www.abcactionnews.com/dpp/news/region_south_pinellas/st_pete_beach/man-confesses-to-murdering-his-friend%2C-former-st.-pete-resident-in-panama

Man confesses to murdering his friend, former St. Pete resident in Panama
www.abcactionnews.com
Tampa Bay News, Weather, Radar, Sports and Entertainment
August 18, 2010 at 6:55pm

### August 19th, 2010 I sent an email to Mary

Sent: Thursday, August 19, 2010 5:39 PM
Subject: Re: Newspaper article

hey mary,
just getting time to right back. i have had reporters here at the house everynight. today tina & the C.s will be coming in to st pete airport at 8:15 so i am picking them up and taking them to the motel that cher's friend Paula has. i also was told that don will be here for the service. i'm so thankful for that. Dave is flying in tomorrow. i'm with you he did not kill cher. he feels sooooo bad. he deserves to be at the service. i know they were seperated but that doesn't matter to me. cher loved him and i know he loves her. it really doesn't matter to me what my dad thinks. he didn't want to come see me when i was staying at Alice's. said he had issues with me. well who is supposed to be the parent.

i'm tired of begging him to love me. i don't need to be hurt like that. i love you and i am so very thankful for you. we will be filming the service and it will most likely be on tv but i will make sure you get a copy of the video. wish you could be here but i know you are in spirit.

## A SISTER'S PROMISE

love you mary and can't wait to see you again and spend some more fun times. i love hanging out with you. love judy

## AUGUST 20TH, 2010 I posted a face book message to everyone

the service for cher is CASUAL.shorts are fine. i'm wearing sundress. we are celebrating her life. Bring flip flops we are walking to the water at sunset. ceremony starts at 6:00 so if you want to come early we are there at 5:00. don is here and we spoke to him last night for hours. he is a wonderful man for helping us. thank everyone
August 20, 2010 at 1:14pm

## August 20th, 2010 a picture posted to Cher's face book wall from Julie

SISTERS...—with Cher Hughes and Judy August 20, 2010 at 2:42pm

## JUDY BARBER

### August 21, 2010

Story of Cher is in the St. Petersburg Times newspaper Saturday edition
HER FAMILY AND HER DOG WOULDN'T LET HER VANISH
St. Petersburg Times; Aug 21, 2010; pg. A.1;

### August 21, 2010

I held a service for Cher at the Don Cesar. We did not have Cher's ashes but we did have her with us in spirit.

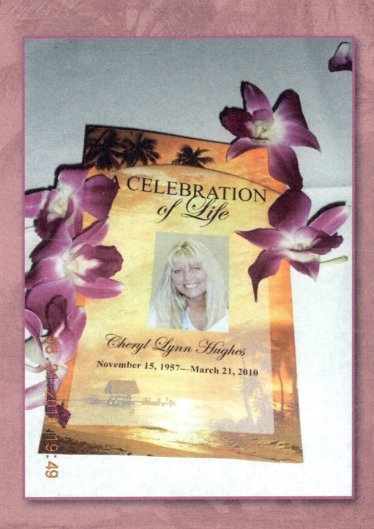

*The Don Cesar the place of Cher's service*

*I had wrote that poem many years ago and sandblasted it onto A mirror for Cher.*

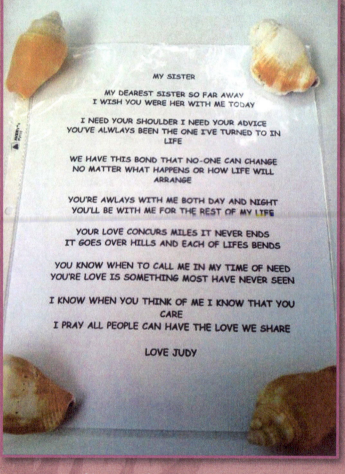

*I wrote this poem after Cher moved to Panama.*
*I missed her so much !!!!!*

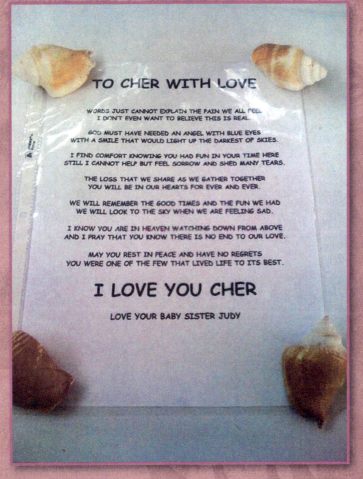

*This poem I wrote as a farewell to my loving sister*

At the end of the service we all walked to the ocean and released 50 white balloons and 3 red heart balloons and flower pedals.

We then gathered at Foxy's restaurant and had the following search
Light shining in the night.

*WE WANTED CHER TO KNOW HOW WE LOVE HER*

### A post to Cher's face book wall from Tammy

Farewell my friend, I will miss you very much. Thank you for all the good times, you will forever be in my memories and embedded deep within my heart. Till we meet again my friend, I love you, Tammy
August 21, 2010 at 10:53pm

### August 24th, 2010 Post made to face book

6:28am
Judy was tagged in Sher O.'s photo.

8:27pm
Judy shared Shawns album: Cher Hughes Memorial Service—St Petersburg, FL.

Cher Hughes Memorial Service—St Petersburg, FL

### August 26th, 2010 Post on face book

August 26
8:06pm
Judy shared Sam's photo.

# JUDY BARBER

Cher Hughes Foundation
8:06pm
Judy shared Sam C's photo.

Cher Hughes Foundation

Cher's backyard, where the kids always were when Cher was home!

## August 30, 2010

The Globe had an article about Cher
ALL-AMERICAN MONSTERS
Carolina Fugitives turn serial killers preying on other Yanks in Panama

## August 31st, 2010 I received an email from Dateline

From: A., Xxx (NBC Universal) [mailto:Xxx. A.@xxxx.com]
Sent: Tuesday, August 31, 2010 10:22 AM
To: judy
Subject: Hi there

Hi Judy,

Thanks so much for chatting with me yesterday, do appreciate you sharing your memories of Cher with me. I did want to reach out to your sister Alice to chat with her for a little bit—when do you think would be a good time for me to call her? If she would rather call me my number at work is xxxxx.

Hope that you were able to get some sleep last night. I'll keep you posted about the interview.

Thanks so much,

Beth

Beth
Dateline NBC
xxx. X.@xxxi.com

### I forwarded the email to my sister Alice

To: Alice
Sent: Tuesday, August 31, 2010 7:29 PM
Subject: judy

hey sis,
i talked with dateline a litte more last night and she wanted to know if she could speak with you. i didn't want to give her your number so i am forwarding her number to you.

give me a call when you get a chance. i'd like to know if any thing else has happened.
love ya know your busy.

### September 3rd, 2010 a post to Cher's face book wall from Melissa

## JUDY BARBER

It was such an honor to be a guest at your Beautiful Home! Thank you for the memories I will have for a life time!
September 3, 2010 at 9:26pm

### September 9th, 2010 8:46pm I posted a comment on face book

I could not believe that the killer was granted phone privileges and he was complaining of his living conditions to a news station in North Carolina. REALLY!!!!!
Judy commented on a link.
WLOS ABC 13 News :: Raw News—Holbert Jail Interview
www.wlos.com
"I DON'T EVEN BELIEVE THIS. I AM SOOOOOOO ANGRY RIGHT NOW. I CAN'T UNDERSTAND HOW THIS SICK IDIOT EVEN GETS TO TALK ON THE PHONE. POOR THING CAN'T TALK TO HIS WIFE!!!!! GIVE ME A CALLING CARD TO TALK TO MY SISTER YOU SON OF A B----!"

### September 9, 2010 I sent out a face book email

HOW IS THIS ALLOWED TO HAPPEN!!!
Holbert was able to get an interview in prison. He is actually complaining
about the conditions in which he is living.

WLOS ABC 13 News :: Raw News—Holbert Jail Interview
www.wlos.com
WLOS ABC 13 News :: Raw News—Holbert Jail Interview—Holbert Jail Interview
September 9, 2010 at 8:48pm

## ~~~September 9th, 2010 I sent an email to the family

Sent: Thursday, September 9, 2010 9:03 PM
Subject: judy

hi everyone,
i just got off the phone with dateline again. they want me to go to new york and interview about cher. after just getting on face book after a few days and listening to that phone interview with the killer. i am thinking about going. i want to fight to keep them two as miserable as possible. how do we defend cher and make sure there are no plea deals?

i have spoken with Xxx at dateline three times now. she is a very nice lady and when i talked to her tonight even she said that what i have told her about cher that it's hard to imagine this kind of thing happening.

i want the world to know who he killed. cher was not just an object she was a wonderful person. i would like for you guys to give me your opinion. do you think it would be a good idea to go on dateline. maybe if we get them involved it might help with getting information.

i am going to talk to xxx again on monday. cher is worth fighting for and if this would help in any way I AM THERE.

love ya all
Judy

## ~~~September 10th, 2010 I received an email from Mary

From: mary
Subject: Re: judy
To: "Judy

## JUDY BARBER

Date: Friday, September 10, 2010, 9:42 AM

Go. Yes. Go. Love Mary

### September 10th, 2010 I received an email from Thomas my brother in law

From: THOMAS
To: 'Judy
Sent: Friday, September 10, 2010 8:23 AM
Subject: RE: Judy

Judy,
If you think that going to New York to give an interview will help you find some peace… I say… go for it. It certainly can't hurt to get the family's of the victims a little media attention. I also listened to Holbert's interview… with him whining about his human rights being violated… just makes me sick. I did however… get some satisfaction knowing that he is getting abused every single day… living in the worst of conditions.

I would not worry about any plea deals for him or his girlfriend. Holbert did mention in his interview that there were others involved with the murders besides him and his girlfriend, so if they were to get a reduced sentence for giving up the names of anyone else involved, it would be worth the trade. I just hope that he lives long enough to reveal the identity of his accomplices, so they too can be brought to justice and punished for their crimes. Whether Holbert and Reese or their accomplices are sentenced to 50 years or less… I seriously doubt that any of them survive long enough to serve out their entire sentence. Eventually, they will either get sick and die from some disease, or die at the hands of another prisoner, or maybe even one of the guards will beat them to death. Don't know and really don't care as long as they are all suffering every second of every day until they are all dead. Do I sound bitter…? Maybe just a little…

Anyway, whatever helps you heal and find some peace… make it happen.

Love Ya,

## September 10th, 2010 I received and email from Alice my sister

From: Alice
To: 'Judy
Sent: Friday, September 10, 2010 7:46 PM
Subject: RE: Judy

Random thoughts from my head:
I thought you were concerned about showing your face to the public and Holbert/Reese families?
I think it depends on what your fighting for or about. Cher was definitely a good person and a very giving and teaching person. WE (friends and family) know who she was and what she was all about.
What can you say to a reporter that is going to let the Panama police/government know that Holbert and Reese should stay in prison forever?
He gets 50 years for the first 5 in Panama—there will be more found. Another 25 (I think) for the death in Coasta Rica. If he makes it out of Panama prison, he won't make it out of Coasta Rica prison.
Panama police already lied to him about letting Reese go if he confessed but they didn't let her go. They'll lie to him again to get more answers.
They'll starve him and beat him until he tells them everything they can get out of him.

### 🙢 JUDY BARBER

We haven't heard how Reese is doing in the prison system yet. Wish they would interview her. She's so stupid, listening to Holbert... she gets 50 years for not talking—ha ha ha. And the more people they find the more time she will get too.

You can tell them I will not be contacting them. I still keep my guns close by and installed a new alarm system a couple weeks ago. I'm still afraid of crazy assholes that want to make a name for themselves by being a copycat or joining his cause.
If you go only use mom, dad, sister, brother but please do not use our names.
Let me know if you go and when it'll be aired so I can see you on tv.

I Love You Bunches, please be careful
Alice

## SEPTEMBER 10TH I received a face book message from Thomas

Judy... We heard through the grapevine that Holbert's mother bought him the cell phone and Holbert's lawyer gave it to him. Sounds to me like God has already passed judgement on Holbert and Reese and has sent them both to HELL ON EARTH. Hope they both suffer every second of every day until they are both dead. Then they can both BURN IN HELL FOR ETERNITY...!
September 10, 2010 at 4:05am

## September 12, 2010 I sent an email to Mary

Sent: Sunday, September 12, 2010 11:24 AM
Subject: Re: judy

thanks mary,i just don't know what to do with myself. there isn't a minute of a day that goes by that i don't think of cher and how lucky i was to have her in my life. i have this hole in my heart that just aches all the time. i am doing my best to take each day one at a time but sometimes one day seems too much. i will keep you posted and let you know when i talk to dateline again on monday. i love yu and thanks for being my friend.

## September 15th, 2010 pictures posted to Cher's face book wall from Trent

*With Cher Hughes*

Cher "catching" a bird

Cher on way to island

## JUDY BARBER

### September 15th, 2010 I received an email from Dateline

From: , J (NBC Universal) [mailto:xxxr.@nxxxxi.com]
Sent: Wednesday, September 15, 2010 5:41 PM
Subject: Dateline NBC / Tampa—NYC / ITINERARY—Updated

Hi Doug and Judy,

Attached are your travel itineraries for the Dateline NBC interview in New York.

We have booked you seats on a 6:55pm JetBlue flight out of Tampa International Airport tomorrow evening, flying into JFK Airport. An NBC car will take you to your hotel—the driver will be at the JFK baggage claim holding a sign with Judy's name on it.

You will be staying at the Hilton hotel in midtown Manhattan—the reservation is under Doug's name.

June will bring a makeup artist to your hotel room ahead of your interview on Friday morning. All further details for the day are in the attached itinerary.

On Saturday, an NBC car will pick you up at 2:00pm from the Hilton hotel and take you to JFK Airport. Your American Airlines return flight will depart from JFK Airport at 4:30pm and arrive in Tampa at 7:40pm.

IMPORTANT: I have also forwarded you online ticket confirmations—please print these out and bring with you when you check in at the airport.

Thank you and have a safe flight,

## September 16, 2010

Flew to New York to do interview with Dateline NBC returned on September 18, 2011. Stayed at the Hilton.
Left tampa 6:55 pm arrived new york 9:34 pm

I never thought my first trip to New York would be to talk about the murder of my sister. I was very over whelmed by how Cher's story had spread so far.

## September 17, 2010 I was interviewed by Kate Snow with Dateline.

*Mary had a layover in New York and was able to meet us at the interview.*

## JUDY BARBER

### September 17, 2010 a post to Cher's face book wall from Tammy

Miss you Cher!
September 17, 2010 at 11:42pm

Left new york September 18, 2010
4:30 pm arrive in tampa 7:40 pm

### September 19, 2010 a post to Cher's face book wall from Alice

I miss you!
September 19, 2010 at 11:37am

### September 23, 2010 I posted on face book to everyone

went to new york last thursday and interviewed with dateline about cher. they are going to do an hour show about her. i was happy to get to share some of my memories of her. it's still so hard to deal with. i miss her so much. they are going to air the show sometime in october. i will let you know when i know for sure what day. they were very kind & caring. i just want the world to know what a great person she was and what a lose we are suffering. for now i am just taking life one day at a time.
September 23, 2010 at 7:18pm

### September 26th, 2010 a post to Cher's face book wall from Tammy

I just got done going through some of my old e-mails and came across some of our old conversations. I will miss you forever my dear friend, I am so glad that I have so many good memories of all the fun we

had. You always made my life brighter and put a smile on my face. I am sure that you are up in heaven dancing with the angels, spreading your wings and sharing that contagious smile of yours. Kiss my mom, till we meet again, I love you, Tammy
September 26, 2010 at 12:20am

## October 1st, 2010 7:23 a.m. I posted a comment on face book to everyone

ANOTHER INTERVIEW THAT WILD BILL WAS ABLE TO DO WITH THE NEWS STATIONS

WLOS ABC 13 News :: Raw News—Holbert Jail Interview www.wlos.com

"they are still getting better treatment then they deserve. they have destroyed too many peoples lifes. cher will be heard sometime in october she will be on dateline. i will let everyone know. the world is going to find out what this animal and his wife did and who they took from us. it's sickening to even know he has the right to talk. they should cut out his tongue so he will stop whining. and his wife should have her ears cut off for wearing cher's earings. send them as gifts to each other so they have something to hold on to. it's more than we have."

## October 5th, 2010 Mary sent an email to Alice

Alice,
What date is Henrys b'day? Dateline is asking and Judy doesn't know.
Mary

## JUDY BARBER

## October 5th, 2010 Mary forwarded me an email from Alice

From: Alice
Date: Tue, Oct 5, 2010 at 8:26 AM
Subject: Re: Henry's birthday
To: mary

Judy does not have permission to give out any information regarding my dad or myself. She was told this in an email before she decided to talk to Dateline.
I left her a voice msg and sent her a text.


Sent: Tuesday, October 5, 2010 12:27 PM
Subject: Fwd: Henry's birthday

She is her mother all over again. I actually laughed out loud. Mean & stupid!
Mary

From: Scott
To: Mary ;Judy
Sent: Tuesday, October 5, 2010 5:52 PM
Subject: RE: Henry's birthday

no secret
His date of birth is xx/xx/xx per public Records.
Scott

Date: Tue, 5 Oct 2010 15:47:50 – 0700
From: Judy
Subject: RE: Henry's birthday
To: mary; Scott

LOL boy did i ever get a nasty message and then a text. all dateline wanted to know is what month dad's bday is because i said in the interview that cher always called dad on his birthday and we really knew something was wrong when she didn't call. i don't think cher would be too happy about the way we are being treated. i would love to move to panama and run her motel and build a school for the children. cher opened a door to paradise for her family and friends to enjoy and i want to carry that on for her. i would already be living there if this would not of happened to cher. i just hate how money can change people. i sure don't know what Alice is so upset about. what about all the hard work that both of you did to help find cher. i guess that has been forgotten by some but not by me. i truely am thankful for what you guys did and for the respect that you showed for cher. i love her & miss her so much and i want her to be proud of what she had accomplished just like i wanted to tell the world. why shouldn't the world hear from a victims point of view? i love you both and i will keep you posted on my punishment. LOL Love Judy

## October 5th, 2010 Mary sent me an email

From: mary
To: Judy
Sent: Tuesday, October 5, 2010 10:10 PM
Subject: Fwd: Contact information for Cheryl Hughes' sister/father

Judy,
This email shows Alice confusing the procedings...I feel she was making us look stupid.

---------- Forwarded message ----------
From: Panama, ACS <xxxx@state.gov>
Date: Tue, Aug 10, 2010 at 8:18 AM
Subject: RE: Contact information for Cheryl Hughes' sister/father

## JUDY BARBER

To: Alice
Cc: mary , "Panama, ACS" <xxx@state.gov>

Good morning, Ladies:

I visited the fiscal handling Cher's murder case yesterday at 2:30 to explain the process the Embassy used to collect DNA when one relative was in the United States, in hopes of persuading him to use a similar method so that neither Mary nor Alice would need to travel to Panama. He responded by telling me that Dave had been in that morning and had told him that Mary was to have arrived yesterday afternoon.

Perhaps one of you could pass Dave's email so I can do my part to make sure that I am better informed as to your plans.

Thank you,

xx


This email is UNCLASSIFIED.

From: xx(Panama)
Sent: Friday, August 06, 2010 3:50 PM
To: , Howard E (Panama)
Cc: Alice
Subject: Contact information for Cheryl Hughes' sister/father

Howard,

I just received a call from Ms. Alice (ccd above in email), the sister of Cheryl Hughes whom we met with along with the aunt Mary and husband Dave.

Alice indicated that she should be the family member, acting for her father, that provides DNA, etc, and works with the Consulate and the Panamanian officials to positively identify and repatriate Cheryl's remains. I explain to her that this was a function of the Consul General's Office and the American Citizen Services, so I would defer to you. I did take the liberty to explain that you were verifying with the Panamanian Authorities if Cheryl's "blood" relatives could furnish their DNA samples in the US, and have them shipped via FedEx, etc., to Panama.

Please let me know if I can be of assistance,

xx III
FBI Legal Attaché
US Embassy Panamá

Mary sent me another email

From: mary
To: Judy
Sent: Tuesday, October 5, 2010 10:20 PM
Subject: Fwd: Cher Hughes—we are in Panama

Judy,
Read this from top to bottom and it is self explanitory, but if you have questions I will answer them. Note the dates, I tried to keep this quiet, but felt I had to advise Dave after Alice told him he didn't have her permission to go on her Dad's property. It still makes me angry—Dave could be in jail right now trying to prove he is innocent.
Mary

---------- Forwarded message ----------
From: mary
Date: Thu, Aug 26, 2010 at 8:03 PM

## JUDY BARBER

Subject: Fwd: Cher Hughes— we are in Panama
To: Dave

------- Forwarded message ----------
From: mary
Date: Sat, Aug 14, 2010 at 11:14 AM
Subject: Fwd: Cher Hughes—we are in Panama
To: JIM ,Scott , Sam , James

Hi Guys,
I just found this email.

I was in the shower when Alice sent this email. I had signed onto my email and suggested Alice email Henry & Thomas that we had arrived safely to Panama. I asked her to confirm our appointment with Howard the US Embassy Consul General. I did not hear the phone conversation either. Remember at this point, we had not spoken with the Police Officials, the investigation had not started. I was under the disillusion that Howard was going to provide assistance.

Alice makes accusations of Dave, to an American Official, in my name.

She is subverting a murder investigation!! She signed my name, only my name, as she knew I had credibility and she didn't. If she convinces officials that Dave is not legal, maybe complicit in this crime, she hopes to have Henry be the beneficiary, in turn she gets the power and $$$.

At this moment, I KNEW Bill Cortez was the suspect, we did not KNOW Cher was dead. I had spoken directly to Alice NOT TO CONTAMINATE our united front.

Luckily, Howard is an idiot. Alice and he are right now still having ongoing communication, but that is just Idiot 1 speaking with Idiot 2 and they can simply entertain one another.

Howard did forward this to the FBI Agent, before our meeting. Now I know why Patty was confused at our meeting—because what this email said and what I was saying at the meeting were polar opposite. I looked like a fool.

Luckily, Alice's backstabbing had no real effect. However, I had to read this email 3 times to truly comprehend it. I am totally shocked. I will not share this with Dave or anyone else unless Alice forces the issue. I will not even advise Alice that I have found this email. I am not going to correct this with Howard or Patty. I have forwarded this to my four brothers. I want this to remain confidential, but needed to share what has happened. Alice & Thomass' actions in the last few weeks now makes more sense. I spoke with Henry (not about this), but I believe he is clueless and Alice is merely using him as a front.

Mary

---------- Forwarded message ----------
From: Howard (Panama) < Fxx@state.gov>
Date: Mon, Jul 12, 2010 at 9:21 AM
Subject: RE: Cher Hughes—we are in Panama
To: "Panama, ACS" <xxx@state.gov>, mary


Paris, ACS:

I called the room and spoke with Alice, Cher's sister, who is staying in the same room as Mary W. Alice explained that Dave and Cher had lived together but that she, Alice, suspected that they never filed the paperwork to make their marriage official. There was a ceremony. 5 years ago. At the end of September 2009, Dave announced he

## JUDY BARBER

was leaving her. Alice alleges that Dave was cheating on her with a younger woman.

Alice is really concerned about Cher's bank account. I reemphasized the likelihood that they would need a lawyer and reiterated that I could not recommend one. I also suggested that if they want to talk to me without Dave, that they simply say so and ask him to leave so we can continue on.
Mf
SBU
This email is UNCLASSIFIED.

From: Panama, ACS
Sent: Monday, July 12, 2010 7:39 AM
To: 'mary
Subject: RE: Cher Hughes— we are in Panama

Welcome to Panama.

My appointment with you is at 11:30. I won't be speaking to the press nor do I think they'll be admitted, certainly not by me. I'll give you a call in a few hours so as to allow you a chance to sleep in a little.

xxx
This email is UNCLASSIFIED.

This is the email the Alice sent from Mary's computer

From: mary Sent: Monday, July 12, 2010 7:12 AM
To: Howard (Panama)
Subject: re:Cher Hughes—we are in Panama

Mr XXXXX

We are here in Panama today, are we still meeting on Tuesday at 11:30 or did it change to Monday and what time? we received a phone call from Dave (supposed husband) wanting to bring the press on Monday. The press is with Dave not with me. We are unsure that a marriage certificate was filed with the civil courts in Panama and do not wish to discuss certain items with Dave. We will play his game until we can find out if he is
(by law) Cher's husband because we still need info from him.

Please confirm our meeting with you.
We are staying at the Marriott in Panama City xxx, room xxx if you would like to call.
Thank you
Mary

## October 6th, 2010 I received an email from Scott

From: Scott
Subject: RE: Henry's birthday
To: "Judy
Date: Wednesday, October 6, 2010, 8:33 AM

Just take the high road, Judy.
You did nothing wrong. And the small things are not worth your time and
energy.
Just egnor it , do not respond to negativitly as it just draws you in, and there is no good out come.
Time will tell... just let it go.

Make "yourself" happy first.
love ya
"uncle" Scott

## ✿ JUDY BARBER

I emailed Scott back

Sent: Wednesday, October 6, 2010 11:41 AM
Subject: RE: Henry's birthday

you are right Scott. i have better things to do with my time then to get caught up in the drama. i have been a distant person for many years and with all that is going on and speaking to mary last night i feel much better about myself. thanks for your support.

love ya
Judy

I CANNOT STOP THINKING ABOUT GOING TO PANAMA.
HOW CAN I GET THERE? I remembered I had not used my original ticket to Panama. I thought it would not hurt to ask if I could exchange that ticket. I sent an email to Expedia.

To: Expedia Travel Services <usmail@expediamail.com>
Sent: Wednesday, October 6, 2010 12:43 PM
Subject: Re: Expedia travel confirmation—Panama City, Panama—May 02, 2010—(Itin# xxxxxx)

i have a question, i never got to use my ticket to go to panama because my sister that i was going to visit went missing. we found out she was killed by a serial killer. i'm not sure if
this was a non refundable ticket or if i can use it for future travel. i just thought i would ask.
i do have intentions of going to panama to see the paradise that my sister lived in.
can you please let me know if there is anything i can do.

thank you
Judy B

I emailed twice to be sure

To: Questions, Refund
Subject: Question about the refund process

To whom it may concern,

My name is Judy Barber and I am writing this letter in reference to an airline ticket that I had purchase on April 4, 2010 for a trip to Panama on May 2nd to see my sister Cheryl Hughes. My sister had lived in Panama for 9 years and this was to be my first visit to see her. Unfortunately my sister went missing and I never was able to use the ticket. We found out that she had been murdered by a serial killer. There are many articles that I can submit as proof of this horrible event. Here is just one website
http://www.baynews9.com/article/news/2010/august/138160/

I am wanting to go to Panama to see the place that made my sister so happy. Her birthday would have been November 15th. It was suggested to me that since I did not use my ticket in May that there may be a chance that I could use the ticket in November. I am asking if this could be considered due to the circumstances.

## ~~~~October 15th I received a response regarding my ticket

From: Questions, Refund <Refund.Questions@aa.com>
Subject: FW: Question about the refund process
To: Judy
Date: Friday, October 15, 2010, 1:57 PM

Ms. B
I am so sorry to hear about your sister.
Can you possibly scan a copy of something that indicates you are her

## JUDY BARBER

sister? I do have the article but it does not indicate family member names on it.
If you had a service for her, perhaps your name was mentioned on something that had to do with the service?
Thank you,
xxxx


Sent: Friday, October 15, 2010 11:51 AM
To: Questions, Refund
Subject: Re: FW: Question about the refund process

thank you for your quick response.
i have attached the page from the booklet from the service that states my name as sister.
please let me know if you received this and if it will be sufficient.

thank you again
Judy

From: Questions, Refund <Refund.Questions@aa.com>
Subject: RE: FW: Question about the refund process
To: "Judy B
Date: Friday, October 15, 2010, 5:02 PM

Mrs. Barber:
Thank you for providing this document.
I have issued a credit for $332.70 to the account
Thank you,
xxx

To: RefundQuestions <Refund.Questions@aa.com>
Sent: Friday, October 15, 2010 1:21 PM
Subject: RE: FW: Question about the refund process

# A SISTER'S PROMISE

thank you so much. i will be booking a flight to panama with american airlines. i really appreciate the help. Judy B

Wow what a relief I now know how I can get to Panama. I had spoken to Dave and he was getting Cher's ashes. I asked him to please wait for me so I can attend
The service at her island. I had made her a promise and wanted to make sure I kept it.

## October 18, 2010

Booked my flight with Air Panama for November 5 2010 – November 20, 2010

American airlines
November 5th 2010 left tampa 7:00 am arrive maimi 8:00 am
Leave miami 9:45 am arrive panama city 11:40 am

Return flight Saturday November 20, 2010
Leave panama city 4:00 pm arrive miami 7:00 pm
Leave miami 10:15 pm arrive tampa 11:15 pm

## October 19, 2010 I sent a face book message to everyone

i just received confirmation that dateline will be showing cher story this friday 22nd at 10 pm
October 19, 2010 at 1:05pm ·
October 22, 2010
Dateline NBC: Stealing Paradise

## October 23rd, 2010 1:05 a.m. Shawn posted a face book message to everyone

Dateline NBC: Stealing Paradise—View the entire story that aired Oct. 22, 2010
www.msnbc.msn.com

## October 23rd, 2010 I received an email from Dave

From: Dave
To: Judy
Sent: Saturday, October 23, 2010 12:35 PM
Subject: NBC Dateline

Xxx,
Your show on Cher was well done indeed, you did her memory justice. I am so appreciative of the detail in which you told her story and the history of our life together. I know her family is proud of your

portrayal of the wonderful person she was and her many accomplishments. I will forever be thankful to you for that.

Your piece on Bill himself was a disappointment, you should have checked for current developments. I found out this week that the evidence, not the rantings of a madman tell a different story. He bound and tortured the entire Brown family, most likely tortured the boy or wife until Mr brown gave up the location of his assets, shot him in the head and then cut his head off and took out his teeth. Bo as well was treated to the same. Cher was not looking at animals but rather was executed on his boat. Laura is a confirmed accomplice in the killings who is being charged as such.

The entire white supremacy aspect of his life and video we all saw was an important element of this monsters persona, was also left untold. All of these facts were given to a writer from the states last week by the prosecutor and you too could have easily obtained these important facts before airing your piece.

You told the world that he said I hired him to kill my wife, yet did not bother to impress the fact that without my accusing him of murder he would still be out there killing people.

The fact that it was me that told the police about the AK 47 that allowed them to execute a search warrant on the property was left out as well. Your quote from me was nothing more than a simple dismissal, when you asked me for a quote, I told you all of the above. Why would I go through so much time and expense to unsure my supposed "Hitman" be captured and brought to justice.

You portrayed Bocas as nothing more than a party town full of drunks and criminals, when in fact most of us here either came to make a life for ourselves or retire in peace in a beautiful place most can only dream of.

I have received many e mails and calls due to your lack of professionalism.

I did my best to aid you and NBC to bring this horrific story to the world and you have left me as well as my family open to unfair judgement. I know it's to late, but felt it was necessary to express my my deep sorrow that NBC has allowed this monster to continue to cause myself and family pain. I will forward this e mail to those friends and family members affected by your broadcast and ask them to due the same until it becomes viral, unless you can find some way to undo some of the damage you have allowed to be done.

Dave

### October 27th, 2010 I received the translated death certificate.

Cher died due to a cerebral laceration, struck in the head by a projectile from a firearm. I could not believe that I was reading this. How could this happen. What kind of monster would shoot my sister in the head? How could Cher by dead? Please Please let me wake up.

### November 1st, 2010 a post to Cher's face book wall from Humberto

we miss you dear friend..
November 1, 2010 at 7:55pm

### NOVEMBER 5TH, 2010 I LEFT FOR PANAMA

I went to panama for the first time November 5, 2010 and it was not for the reason that I wanted. It was to bury Cher on her island and bring her ashes
back to united states. It was devastating. To try and enjoy being in the foreign paradise I heard so much about was not possible. I had a job to do, a mission to accomplish. A long time friend of cher's Mark traveled with me so at least I was
not alone.

## JUDY BARBER

I had the honor of meeting Jack and I could say that I felt the love he had for my sister. Jack was staying with a friend of Cher's and I went there on my trip. As I was sitting on the porch, Cher's friend opened the door and out walked Jack. I must say that I am usually a little afraid of big dogs, but for some reason I was not afraid at all. Jack locked eyes with me from the moment he saw me. I know he knew who I was. He walked over to me and put his head right on my lap. He leaned on me as if to ask to be held. Without any hesitation I hugged him with everything I had and told him that Cher was proud of him.

That moment was like no other experience I have ever had. I had a connection with a strange dog but yet he was not a stranger at all. I could see why Cher was so attached to him. I could see the hurt in his face and the pain in his eyes. He lost a friend, a mother and someone that he obviously loved very deeply. I know this all might seem like I am wanting to embellish the story but this is the actual truth. I went to see the place that Cher always went to pray. It was truly beautiful

## ⁓⁓⁓November 8th, 2010 I emailed my husband and daughter

From: Judy
To: jen
Sent: Monday, November 8, 2010 7:54 AM
Subject: mom

hi guys,finally got to a computer that will work. staying at cher's friends house since we got here. been raining everyday but ok. will probably go to the motel cher had and stay a couple days there. everyone very nice have meet a few of cher's friends. went to a few different bars and had a drink for cher. this is really strange being here without here. i do my best to appreciate it and try not to cry. i wish cher was here it would make such a difference for me. we are safe and in good hands. have seen lots of beautiful scenery here. miss you and love you so much. tell everyone ok and i will try and contact you soon. don ;t know if it's the rain messing with computers or phones but i have tried to send a bunch of messages on my phone and it keeps saying will save message until service is available. please be safe and take of yourself. i miss you guys and love you so much. i will write you soon. i will try and get on face book and post so everyone knows I'm ok. love yas

*I stayed at Cher's motel for a few days.*

*I walked the island of Carenaro to find the school children that meant so much to Cher.*

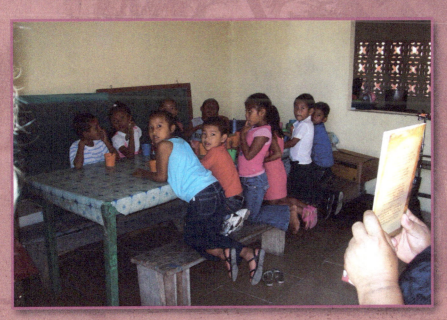

*I found the school and a lot of the children knew Cher. I was amazed at the Hugs I received from them. It was Cher that was always trying to help these children and now they are comforting me.*

*It was sad to see what some of these children call home. I understand what Compelled Cher to want to help.*

A SISTER'S PROMISE

*While walking the island I came across a concrete path covered with butterflies.*

This to me was priceless. Ever since Cher passed I have been seeing butterflies.


On November 14, 2010 I saw her island for the first time. I went there to prepare for the service the next day which would have been her 54th birthday. I really cannot even put into words how I felt. I just wanted to wake up from the worst nightmare I could imagine. Cher was with me but she was in a pink box. I held onto her ashes so damn tight and I just wanted to scream over and over again. I did my best to hold myself together. I wanted to honor my sister and hope and pray that she would know that I was there.

*My first glimpse of the private island that Cher called her paradise.*

*The spot for Cher's ashes was dug.*

*She will always be able to see the view of the water.*

*We placed flowers around the hut. Cher always loved flowers.*

I went through a hope chest that was filled with photos that Cher had taken over the years.

*Cher as a baby!!!!*

## JUDY BARBER

We gathered on the island on November 15, 2010 and had a real nice services. It was small but meaningful. We each said a few words about cher and we buried her ashes. We each took a bite of an apple and then planted the apple Core. Cher's favorite drink was an apple martini. We had hoped the apple would grow and cher could have her apple martini whenever she wanted. When we left the island I just felt so emotional. I could not fill the emptiness In my heart. I was thankful to have at least full filled part of the promise I had made to Cher.

## JUDY BARBER

I could not help but fall apart when we left the island. Jack was right by my side as if he knew I needed comforting. I felt his sorrow as he felt mine. He kept looking back at the island. I knew he did not want to leave.

A SISTER'S PROMISE

## ⁓November 15th, 2010 post to Cher's face book wall

HAPPY BIRTHDAY CHER....Mark is up there with you now so you have a fishing buddy! I miss you girl....LOVE YOU 4EVER.....
November 15, 2010 at 9:08pm ·Julie

Alice
Happy Birthday Sissy!!! I love you and miss you very much.
November 15, 2010 at 8:16pm

## ⁓November 16th, 2010 a post to Cher's face book wall from Sam

Cher's god father

Happy birthday Cher, Just went through about 200 pictures or more

## JUDY BARBER

from our trips to Panama , That was some of the best times And remembering your visits at the lake here.Will be seeing you again. Hold a spot for Anne and I. I'm sure your Island up there Is beautiful beyond description. Watch over your family and friends.Till we meet again Love you
November 16, 2010 at 8:57pm

### November 16th, 2010 There was a parade in Bocas

It seemed kind of ironic. I joked with Cher's friends that the parade was for her.

We all knew Cher enjoyed a crowd.

A SISTER'S PROMISE

I know Cher would have enjoyed watching these children.

### November 17th, 2010 a post to Cher's face book wall from Tammy

Happy Belated Birthday my dear friend. I think about you often and miss you greatly. Kiss my loved ones and hold them tight as I know that they will with you. You are always on my mind and forever in my heart. Love you Lady, Tammy XOXOXOX
November 17, 2010 at 11:28am

### November 20th, 2010 I left panama and returned to Florida

I packed some of Cher's ashes to take home. I had to do as I promised. Before I left panama our cab driver Roger, whom was Cher's driver for years, took us for a drive to see the sites.

*Panama City*

A SISTER'S PROMISE

*I passed this butterfly on the way to the top. I knew Cher was with me.*

## November 21st, 2010 I sent an email to Mary and Scott

To: mary ; Scott
Sent: Sunday, November 21, 2010 12:30 PM
Subject: judy
Hey Mary & Scott
just wanted to let you know i made it back safely. i got in town at 11:30 last night. we had a wonderful service for cher on the island. planted a tree in her honor and put her to rest.
i was able to get some of her ashes and i have them here with me. i meet a lot of nice people, saw the children at the school. Dave took me and Mark to a lot of places. it was good for me but i cried a lot just picturing how & what cher would of said about each place. i feel good for doing what i set out to accomplish for cher. thanks for the

## JUDY BARBER

encouragement and love. i will post some pictures later any way just wanted to let you know i'm ok. i'm still jet lagged and got lots to do to go to work tomorrow. i love you.
love judy

### November 25, 2010 I sent a face book message to everyone

HAPPY THANKSGIVING EVERYONE. i hope everyone enjoys their day. i am thankful to be able to complete my promise to cher today. on her birthday i was in panama to help put her to rest on her island and today we will be putting her to rest on Sunshine Island.i truely am thankful for the time i had with her. may we all find something to be thankful for today. love and best wishes to all November 25, 2010 at 10:58am

I thought it was very odd while writing this that November 25th, 2009 was the day I joined face book and Cher was my first friend.
November 25th, 2009 11:12pm I joined face book to stay in contact with Cher
Judy and Cher Hughes are now friends.

A SISTER'S PROMISE

**November 25th, 2010 I completed my promise to Cher.**

She now has been laid to rest on her island and Sunshine Island. I did what I told her I would do. I hope and pray that she is proud of me.

I MADE HER A PROMISE AND I KEPT IT!

**CHER AT SUNSHINE ISLAND**
May she rest in Peace!

CPSIA information can be obtained at www.ICGtesting.com
Printed in the USA
LVOW05s1426010215

425192LV00002BB/3/P